MARRIAGE, SEPARATION, AND DIVORCE

MARRIAGE, SEPARATION, AND DIVORCE

For wives, husbands, children, and common-law spouses in Ontario

David I. Botnick, LL.B.

Self-Counsel Press
(a division of)
International Self-Counsel Press Ltd.
Canada U.S.A.

Printed in Canada

First edition: October, 1975; Reprinted: June, 1977
Second edition: August, 1979
Third edition: May, 1982; Reprinted: November, 1984
Fourth edition: May, 1987
Fifth edition: March, 1990
Sixth edition: February, 1993
Seventh edition: October, 1994
Eighth edition: August, 1996

Canadian Cataloguing in Publication Data
Botnick, David I., 1957-
    Marriage, separation, and divorce

    (Self-counsel legal series)
    First ed. by Ruth Davidson; 2nd-3rd eds. by Rodica David;
    4th-5th eds. published under title: Marriage and family law in
    Ontario; 6th-7th eds. published under title: Marriage, separation,
    divorce and your rights.
    ISBN 1-55180-073-X

    1. Domestic relations — Ontario — Popular works.　I. Title.
    II. Title: Marriage, separation, divorce and your rights. III. Series.
    KEO213.Z82B67 1996　　346.71301'5　　C96-910329-8
    KF505.ZB3B67 1996

Self-Counsel Press
(a division of)
International Self-Counsel Press Ltd.
1481 Charlotte Road
North Vancouver, British Columbia V7J 1H1

U.S. Address
1704 N. State Street
Bellingham, Washington 98225

CONTENTS

TABLES

SAMPLES

INTRODUCTION

In recent years, our society has changed many of its attitudes toward marriage, separation, and divorce.

Divorce was once considered a tragic option of last resort, but is now so common that one out of every two marriages ends that way. It is also quite common for people to live together without getting married at all.

As attitudes toward family life have changed, the laws affecting the family have changed as well. The Divorce Act, 1985, and the Family Law Act, 1986, are laws enacted by the governments of Canada and Ontario in response to the public demand for quicker, no-fault divorces and a fairer settlement of matrimonial affairs.

Because of these changes in the laws, many people are not aware of the legal consequences that now arise from marriage and separation. The purpose of this book is to acquaint you with these laws and set out your rights and obligations in general terms. As you go through the book, you will also find suggestions for your best course of action when confronted by typical family problems. These suggestions are not a substitute for individual legal advice; however, they may be used as a basis for further discussion with your lawyer.

NOTICE TO READERS

Laws are constantly changing. Every effort is made to keep this publication as current as possible. However, the author, the publisher, and the vendor of this book make no representation or warranties regarding the outcome or the use to which the information in this book is put and are not assuming any liability for any claims, losses, or damages arising out of the use of this book. The reader should not rely on the author or the publisher of this book for any professional advice. Please be sure that you have the most recent edition.

Note: The fees quoted in this book are correct at the date of publication. However, fees are subject to change without notice. For current fees, please check with the court registry or appropriate government office nearest you.

1
MARRIAGE

a. WHAT IS A MARRIAGE?

When two people marry, they enter into a contract, the terms of which are defined by law. This contract contains many important rights and obligations. Among these are the right to financial support, the right to live in the matrimonial home, and the right to an equal division of family property upon separation or the death of one of the marriage partners. If the marriage produces children, each parent has the right to claim custody, child support, or visiting rights. Finally, there is the right to terminate the relationship by divorce. Each of these rights and obligations is discussed in detail in the chapters that follow.

The law makes the assumption that marriage is a form of partnership. Each spouse is assumed to have made an equal contribution to that partnership, and each is entitled to an equal share if the partnership is dissolved.

b. HOW DO I OBTAIN A MARRIAGE LICENCE?

The formalities required for a legally valid marriage are set out in the Marriage Act, a statute of Ontario. To enter into a legally valid marriage, you must first obtain a marriage licence, which may be issued by the clerk of any city or town in Ontario. Once the marriage licence is obtained, you may get married at any time between the third day and the end of the third month following the date the licence was issued.

To obtain a marriage licence, you must meet the following requirements:

(a) Age: You must be at least 18 years old. If you are under 18 but over 16 years of age, a marriage licence may be issued with the written consent of both your parents or your legal guardian.

(b) Mental capacity: A marriage licence will not be issued to any person who lacks the mental capacity to marry because of mental illness or the influence of liquor or drugs.

(c) Dissolution of prior marriage: If you are divorced and want to remarry, you must produce your final decree of divorce (either the original or a certified copy). If your divorce was obtained outside Canada, you will also need a letter from an Ontario lawyer stating that your divorce decree is valid and recognized under the laws of Ontario.

(d) Blood relationships: A man and woman may not be married to each other if they are more closely related by blood than the Marriage Act allows. The forbidden degrees of relationship are listed in the Marriage Act (see Table #1).

c. WHO CAN PERFORM THE MARRIAGE?

If the marriage is to be a religious ceremony, the person performing it must be registered with the Ontario government as a person authorized to solemnize marriages. Generally speaking, priests, ministers, rabbis, or other leaders of established religious bodies are entitled to be registered.

If the marriage is a civil ceremony, it can be performed by any judge or justice of the peace in Ontario.

The marriage must take place in front of at least two witnesses who must sign their names to the marriage register.

TABLE #1
FORBIDDEN BLOOD RELATIONSHIPS

A man may not marry his	A woman may not marry her
1. Grandmother	1. Grandfather
2. Grandfather's wife	2. Grandmother's husband
3. Wife's grandmother	3. Husband's grandfather
4. Aunt	4. Uncle
5. Wife's aunt	5. Husband's uncle
6. Mother	6. Father
7. Stepmother	7. Stepfather
8. Wife's mother	8. Husband's father
9. Daughter	9. Son
10. Wife's daughter	10. Husband's son
11. Son's wife	11. Daughter's husband
12. Sister	12. Brother
13. Granddaughter	13. Grandson
14. Grandson's wife	14. Granddaughter's husband
15. Wife's granddaughter	15. Husband's grandson
16. Niece	16. Nephew
17. Nephew's wife	17. Niece's husband

The relationships in this table include all such relationships, whether by the whole or half blood.

d. WHAT IS A COMMON-LAW MARRIAGE?

At one time marriage was a private affair governed by the common law, or law based on custom and usage. After governments entered the picture by passing legislation, people who lived together without complying with the formal requirements were considered to have a common-law marriage.

Today a common-law marriage simply refers to two people who are living together, but for one reason or another do not wish to get married or are unable to get married. For many years, the laws of Ontario did not recognize common-law marriages, and none of the rights and obligations of a legally valid marriage applied. Common-law relationships are now given some recognition and, under certain circumstances, a common-law spouse may claim financial support from his or her partner. However, unlike a legally married spouse, the rights of a common-law spouse to equal possession of the matrimonial home or to an equal division of family property are not protected (see chapters 5 and 6). Many people are under the impression that common-law spouses now have the same status as married couples. This is not the case at all as you will see in the chapters that follow.

2
SEPARATION

A marriage is a very complex relationship and problems between the spouses are bound to arise from time to time. When the problems become insurmountable, one or both spouses may feel that a separation is the best solution.

Before making this decision, it is important to carefully consider the legal, financial, and emotional consequences of separation. You would be wise to obtain professional counselling before you walk out the door. In many cases, an experienced counsellor may be able to help you and your spouse reconcile. Even if a reconciliation is out of the question, counselling can help you make the many adjustments required when you decide to separate.

a. WHAT IS A LEGAL SEPARATION?

The term "legal separation" has no meaning in Ontario law. A separation is legal as soon as the spouses are living separate and apart and do not intend to resume cohabitation.

However, there are a number of legal rights and obligations that result from a separation. The most common of these are division of family property, possession of the matrimonial home, support obligations, custody of children, and visiting rights. Each of these subjects is dealt with in detail in the following chapters.

These rights and obligations are triggered by separation, not divorce. Even if you are still married, you are entitled to make one or more of the above claims as long as you and your spouse are living separate and apart.

When spouses do separate, they often enter into a written separation agreement, which lists all their respective rights and obligations. This document is frequently what people have in mind when they request a legal separation. However, as pointed out, all separations are legal. The document is required only to resolve the legal issues resulting from the separation (see chapter 3).

b. THE MECHANICS OF SEPARATION

1. Who moves out?

If there is to be a separation, one or both spouses must move out of the matrimonial home. This can sometimes be a problem, as both spouses have an equal right to possession of the home, regardless of who owns it or pays the rent. Accordingly, if you want a separation and your spouse simply refuses to leave, one option is to simply move out yourself. However, if your spouse has been violent or abusive toward you or the children, you may be able to force your spouse out with a court order for exclusive possession of the home (see chapter 5).

2. What can I take when I leave?

The best approach to dividing household contents is to sit down with your spouse and attempt to agree on the items each of you will keep. In most cases, spouses are able to divide their household possessions without the help of lawyers or court applications. The division of property should not be seen as a means of striking back at the other spouse, but merely as a necessary part of the separation.

If you cannot reach an agreement, or your spouse will not discuss it with you, you should begin by taking your personal possessions, including clothing, jewellery, hobby materials, and collections. You may also take any items you owned before the marriage or received as a personal gift or inheritance during the marriage. Finally, you may take about half of the jointly owned items, such as furniture and appliances, acquired by you both during the marriage. If you are leaving with children, you should also take the children's personal property and whatever jointly owned items are required for looking after the children.

3. Should I clean out the bank account?

Bank accounts in the name of one spouse only are the private property of that spouse; the other spouse has no access to these funds after separation. Joint bank accounts generally belong to both spouses equally, unless there is proof that the spouses intended otherwise. Accordingly, you are entitled to withdraw up to half of the balance in the joint account at the time of separation. If you require additional money for your own support or for support of the children, you may draw against your spouse's half of the joint account, provided that it is necessary and within reason. The courts are likely to frown upon a spouse who cleans out a joint bank account as a parting stab.

4. Has the property been divided equally?

The household items and money a spouse takes when he or she leaves the matrimonial home are not necessarily what that spouse is entitled to receive. If one spouse ends up with more money or property than the other after the separation, he or she may be obliged to make an equalizing payment. The equal division of family property can become very complicated (see chapter 6).

c. VIOLENCE OR HARASSMENT BETWEEN SPOUSES

1. What if my spouse assaults me?

Violence between the spouses may begin or increase following a separation. Whether you are separated or not, if your spouse beats you or threatens your life or health, immediately telephone the police. If the police witness the actual assault, or arrive to find one of the spouses badly injured, they will usually make an arrest and lay charges against the offending spouse. Many times, however, the police do not find actual evidence of the assault other than the statement of the complainant, which is often denied by the other spouse. In that instance, the police usually do not lay charges themselves but will help you lay a private charge of assault. This is done by signing a sworn statement before a justice of the peace about the acts of violence.

The police and the Crown attorney's office are under instructions to take cases of domestic violence very seriously. Any charges laid are proceeded with. If convicted, the accused will be subject to a fine or imprisonment. If you change your mind, you cannot simply telephone the police and tell them you do not wish to proceed. Accordingly, you should not lay charges against your spouse unless you are prepared to appear in court and see the matter through.

2. Peace bonds

A spouse who has been assaulted or threatened with assault does not always want the offending spouse to go to jail. If the assault is a first offence, it is usually sufficient to ensure that if the assault is repeated, the offender will be dealt with severely. This is accomplished by requiring the guilty spouse to enter into a recognizance, commonly known as a peace bond.

The peace bond is basically a promise by the accused to keep the peace and demonstrate good behavior for a period of up to 12 months. It can be accompanied by reasonable conditions, such as abstaining from alcohol or not entering the residence of the complainant spouse. If the accused refuses to agree to the peace bond or subsequently breaches its terms, a jail sentence is likely to follow.

Peace bonds are ordered under the Criminal Code by a judge of the Ontario Court (Provincial Division) or a justice of the peace. Before a peace bond can be ordered, the judge or justice must be satisfied that the complainant has reasonable grounds to fear violence from the other spouse.

3. Restraining orders

A restraining order serves basically the same function as a peace bond but comes under the Family Law Act. You may apply to the court for an order restraining your spouse or former spouse from molesting, annoying, or harassing you and your children or communicating with you or the children, except as the order provides.

The court will generally grant the restraining order upon your sworn affidavit attesting to threats or acts of violence or harassment by your spouse.

A person who violates a restraining order can be fined $1 000 and imprisoned for up to three months. If the offence is repeated, the maximum fine increases to $10 000, the jail sentence to two years.

The jurisdiction to grant a restraining order is wider than that of a peace bond. Even if there is no fear of actual violence, the court may grant a restraining order to prevent harassment or unwanted communication from a spouse or former spouse.

3

DOMESTIC CONTRACTS

a. WHAT IS A DOMESTIC CONTRACT?

A domestic contract is a formal written agreement signed by you and your spouse in front of a witness. The agreement outlines your rights and obligations in the relationship and those of your spouse, so that each party knows where he or she stands. The unique feature of a domestic contract is that it overrides the Family Law Act. You and your spouse can therefore make your own family law by entering into a contract.

There are three types of domestic contracts: marriage contracts, cohabitation agreements, and separation agreements. Each one is described below.

Samples of these three contracts are included in this chapter. Keep in mind that the samples are intended only to show you some of the usual terms and phrases to help you formulate your own domestic contact. Each domestic contract is unique and should be tailored to the particular situation. It should contain only the provisions both you and your spouse want and have agreed to.

1. Marriage contracts

A marriage contract is an agreement between a man and a woman who are married or intend to get married (see Sample #1). The agreement may deal with the couple's rights while they are living together, but it usually focuses on what will happen if there is a separation. The agreement covers division of property, support obligations, and other matters necessary for the settlement of your affairs. However, it cannot deal with custody or access to children; nor can it limit one spouse's right to possession of the matrimonial home.

A marriage contract changes how the law will treat division of property and spousal support. Before you can make a decision about a marriage contract, you must be familiar enough with these laws to realize what you may be gaining or giving up by entering the agreement.

As you read this book, carefully consider whether the laws governing your relationship are satisfactory to you and your spouse. If you do not want some of these laws to apply or if you want your relationship to be governed by additional rules, you may provide for this by entering into a marriage contract with your spouse.

The usual reason people want a marriage contract is for protection. You may own a prosperous business or a valuable piece of property that you do not want to divide with your spouse. Or you may have plans to leave your property to your children when you die and you want to limit your spouse's right to make a claim against your estate. In both these cases, you may protect your property by an appropriate provision in a marriage contract.

Another reason for entering into a marriage contract is security. You may be concerned that your spouse will not provide you with proper financial support, so you may wish to have his or her support obligations spelled out in a contract before committing yourself to the relationship.

A third benefit of a marriage contract is certainty. If there is no contract, there is great potential for dispute over countless trivial matters, ranging from who gets the silverware to who pays for the insurance on the car. In the tense atmosphere following a separation, spouses are often unable to resolve these questions amicably. It is helpful to have a pre-existing agreement that settles the matter.

SAMPLE #1
MARRIAGE CONTRACT

THIS IS AN AGREEMENT made the 20th DAY OF OCTOBER, 199_,
BETWEEN:

JOHN DOE,

(hereinafter called the "Husband")

— and —

JANE DOE,

(hereinafter called the "Wife")

1. BACKGROUND:

The Husband and the Wife were married on the 28th day of December, 1985.
Each desires to settle by Agreement all their rights and obligations which they
have or may acquire upon separation, with respect to ownership of their property,
their right to make a claim in respect to property owned by the other, and with
respect to their right to financial support from the other.

2. AGREEMENT:

The Husband and the Wife each agree to be bound by the provisions of this
Agreement.

3. SEPARATE PROPERTY REGIME:

Except as provided in this Agreement, the Husband and the Wife will each
retain sole ownership, control, and enjoyment of all his or her property free from
any claim by the other.

No property owned by the husband or the wife shall constitute net family
property as defined in the Family Law Act.

4. THE MATRIMONIAL HOME:

a) The Husband and Wife acknowledge that their matrimonial home is a
Condominium Unit, municipally known as 111 Southport Avenue, Unit 1, Toronto,
Ontario, and which they own as joint tenants. In the event that the parties separate,
and continue to live separate and apart for a period of not less than 60 days, the
said Condominium Unit shall be sold at fair market value, and the net proceeds
of sale shall be divided equally between the Husband and the Wife.

b) So long as the parties own the matrimonial home, the Husband shall be
responsible for payment of all common expenses and/or maintenance costs in
respect thereto. The Wife will be responsible for payment of all realty taxes in
respect thereto.

c) If during cohabitation, the said Condominium Unit is sold and another
property is acquired and occupied by the Husband and the Wife as their matrimonial home, the provisions of Paragraphs 4 a) and 4 b) will apply to the newly
acquired property, and so on, for any subsequent property so acquired.

5. PERSONAL PROPERTY:

In the event that the parties separate, they agree in relation to their personal property that:

a) The Husband shall be entitled to ownership and possession free of all claim by the Wife of the following items owned by one or both of them:

(i) Tech turntable, receiver, and stereo speakers;

(ii) Relax reclining leather chair;

(iii) Fish tank and accessories;

(iv) Stamp and coin collection;

(v) Funds on deposit in joint account No. 123456 at the Regal Bank of Canada, Branch located at 22 Orangeway, North York.

b) The Wife shall be entitled to ownership and possession free of all claims of the Husband of the following items owned by one or both of them:

(i) All contents of the matrimonial home, save and except the items mentioned in Paragraph 5 a);

(ii) 1982 Honda Civic automobile;

(iii) Canada Savings Bonds Series 536, having a face value of $5 000, and registered jointly in the name of the Husband and Wife.

6. RELEASES:

a) Property:

Except as provided in this Agreement, the Husband and the Wife each release and discharge all rights to any interests in property owned by the other that he or she may acquire under the laws of any jurisdiction and, in particular, under the Family Law Act, 1986, or any successor in the Province of Ontario, including all rights and interests in:

(1) Ownership in property;

(2) Division of property;

(3) Compensation for contributions made directly or indirectly to the acquisition or maintenance of property;

(4) An equalization of net family property under Part 1 of the Family Law Act, 1986;

Without limiting the generality of the foregoing, the Wife expressly releases and waives any claims, rights, demands, or causes of action she may have or acquire for any share in, compensation in respect of, or interest in Plum Plumbing Ltd., or any successor Corporation of which the Husband is a Shareholder, or in which the Husband may have an interest.

b) Estate:

Except as provided in this Agreement, and subject to any right given by the other in his or her Will, the Husband and the Wife each release and discharge all rights that he or she has or may have under the laws of any jurisdiction in the Estate of the other, and in particular:

(1) Under the Family Law Act, 1986, or any successor in the Province of Ontario, to elect to receive a payment from the Estate equalizing the Net Family Property of the Husband and the Wife;

(2) Under the Succession Law Reform Act, or any successor in the Province of Ontario, to share in the Estate of the other upon the other dying intestate or to an allowance or payment as a dependant from the Estate of the other;

(3) Under the Trustee Act or any successor in the Province of Ontario, to act as Executor or Administrator of the Will or the Estate of the other.

c) Support:

The Husband and the Wife each acknowledge that they are fully capable of supporting themselves, both during cohabitation and in the event of a separation, and hereby forever release one another from any obligations to financially support the other.

d) Pension Rights:

In the event of separation or dissolution of the marriage, neither the Husband nor the Wife will apply under the Canada Pension Plan for a division of pension credits.

7. GENERAL:

a) The Husband and Wife will each execute any document or documents reasonably required from time to time, to give effect to the terms and intent of this Agreement.

b) The Husband and Wife each warrant that there are no representations, collateral agreements, or conditions affecting this Agreement, other than as expressed in this Agreement.

c) This Agreement may be amended or varied only by a further Instrument in writing, signed by the Husband and the Wife.

d) The provisions of this Agreement are binding on the respective heirs, executors, administrators, or assigns of the Husband and the Wife.

8. PROPER LAW:

The law governing the interpretation and implementation of this Agreement is the law prevailing from time to time in the Province of Ontario.

9.   SEVERABILITY OF PROVISIONS:

The invalidity or unenforceability of any provision of this Agreement will not affect the validity or enforceability of any other provision, and any invalid provision will be severable.

10.   INDEPENDENT LEGAL ADVICE AND FINANCIAL DISCLOSURE:

The Husband and the Wife each acknowledge, that he or she:

(a) has had independent Legal Advice;

(b) understands his or her rights and obligations under this Agreement;

(c) is signing this Agreement voluntarily; and

(d) has had complete financial disclosure of the assets and liabilities of one another.

TO EVIDENCE THEIR AGREEMENT, the Husband and the Wife have each signed this Agreement under seal.

SIGNED, SEALED, AND   )
DELIVERED   )
)
In the presence of:)
)
J. M. Witness   )   _John Doe_
WITNESS   )   JOHN DOE
)
AB Goode   )   _Jane Doe_
WITNESS   )   JANE DOE

<u>AFFIDAVIT</u>

JUDICIAL DISTRICT OF YORK	)	I, I.M. WITNESS,
	)	of the City of North York,
	)	in the Municipality of
	)	Metropolitan Toronto,
	)	MAKE OATH AND SAY:

1. That I was personally present, and did see the within or annexed Instrument, duly signed, sealed, and executed by John Doe, one of the parties thereto.

2. That the said Instrument was executed by the said party, at North York.

3. That I know the said party.

4. That I am a subscribing witness to the said Instrument.

SWORN BEFORE ME at the	)	
City of North York in the	)	
Municipality of Metropolitan	)	*J. M. Witness*
Toronto, this 20th day of	)	
October, 199_.	)	
	)	
J. M. Commissioner	)	
A Commissioner, etc.	)	

AFFIDAVIT

JUDICIAL DISTRICT OF YORK	)	I, A.B. GOODE, of the
	)	City of North York,
	)	in the Municipality of
	)	Metropolitan Toronto,
	)	MAKE OATH AND SAY:

1. That I was personally present, and did see the within or annexed Instrument, duly signed, sealed, and executed by Jane Doe, one of the parties thereto.

2. That the said Instrument was executed by the said party at North York.

3. That I know the said party.

4. That I am a subscribing witness to the said Instrument.

SWORN BEFORE ME, at the	)
City of North York, in the	)
Municipality of Metropolitan	) *A.B. Goode*
Toronto, this 20th day of	)
October, 199_.	)
	)
J.M. Commissioner	)
A Commissioner, etc.	

The main disadvantage to a marriage contract for some people is their fear that it will become a self-fulfilling prophecy. Many couples find it distasteful to discuss the future breakdown of their marriage as if it were an unavoidable event. A young couple, in particular, tends to believe that their marriage will be a strong one based on love and mutual trust, in which a written contract is both unnecessary and inappropriate. However, if you do not have a marriage contract, the government writes one for you by imposing on you the rights and obligations of the Family Law Act. If you do not want all or part of the Family Law Act to govern your marriage, the only way to avoid it is by entering into a marriage contract.

2. Cohabitation agreements

A cohabitation agreement is a contract between a man and a woman who are living together but are not married to one another (see Sample #2). The nature and purpose of the agreement is similar to a marriage contract. However, the contents differ considerably. For example, the right to an equal share of net family property (discussed in chapter 6) does not exist between unmarried couples. Therefore, an unmarried couple does not usually require an agreement to keep each partner's property free of claims by the other. On the other hand, if unmarried partners want to have automatic rights against each other's property, a cohabitation agreement is necessary.

Although unmarried spouses are not entitled to an equal share of net family property, they may acquire rights in their partner's property if they have contributed to the acquisition or maintenance of that property. These rights are based on the common law of trusts. For example, a common-law wife who has worked for many years on a farm owned by her common-law husband may acquire an interest in that property under the law of constructive trust. If one or both of the spouses in a common-law relationship have property, a cohabitation agreement is important.

SAMPLE #2
COHABITATION AGREEMENT

THIS IS AN AGREEMENT made the 20th day of October, 199_,
BETWEEN:
JOHN BROWN,
(hereinafter called "Brown")
- and -
JANE SMITH,
(hereinafter called "Smith")

1. BACKGROUND:

Brown and Smith have been cohabiting since January 10th, 1985. Each desires to settle by Agreement all their rights and obligations which they have or may acquire with respect to ownership of their property, their right to make a claim in respect to property owned by the other, and with respect to their right to financial support from one another.

2. AGREEMENT:

Brown and Smith each agree to be bound by the provisions of this Agreement.

3. SEPARATE PROPERTY REGIME:

a) all property now held in the name of either Brown or Smith, or subsequently acquired by either one of them, shall belong exclusively to that person, and shall forever be free of any claim by the other.

b) all property now held in the name of both Brown and Smith or subsequently acquired by both of them, shall belong to Brown and Smith, jointly, each as to a 50% interest.

c) In the event that Brown and Smith cease cohabiting, the property which they own jointly shall be divided equally between them.

If they are unable to agree on how the property should be divided, all the jointly owned property shall be sold and the proceeds of sale shall be divided equally between them.

4. PLACE OF RESIDENCE:

a) Brown and Smith acknowledge that they reside in a Condominium Unit municipally known as 12 John Green Blvd., Unit 15, Toronto, Ontario, of which Brown is the sole owner (and which is referred to herein as the "Condominium"). They further acknowledge, that Smith has made no contribution to the acquisition, repair, or maintenance of the Condominium.

b) Brown shall be responsible for all obligations with respect to repair and maintenance, mortgage payments, and taxes on the Condominium.

c) No contribution or rule of law or statutory provision or any other matter, including any resulting, constructive, or applied trust will give Smith any right to interest in the Condominium.

19

d) Smith shall have the right to reside in the Condominium until such time that Brown requests her to leave. Upon being requested to leave, Smith shall vacate the Condominium and shall remove all her personal property contained therein within a period of two weeks from the date of the request.

5. SUPPORT:

Brown and Smith each acknowledge that they are fully capable of supporting themselves now and in the future, and that neither one is responsible to any degree, for the support of the other.

6. RELEASES:

a) Property:

Except as provided in this Agreement, Brown and Smith each release and discharge all rights to any interests in property owned by the other that he or she may acquire under the laws of any jurisdiction, and in particular, under the Family Law Act, 1986, or any successor in the Province of Ontario, including all rights and interests in:

(1) Ownership in property;

(2) Division of property;

(3) Compensation for contributions made directly or indirectly to the acquisition or maintenance of property;

(4) An equalization of Net Family Property under Part 1 of The Family Law Act, 1986;

b) Estate:

Except as provided in this Agreement, and subject to any right given by the other in his or her Will, Brown and Smith each release and discharge all rights that he or she has or may have under the laws of any jurisdiction in the Estate of the other, and in particular:

(1) Under the Family Law Act, 1986, or any successor in the Province of Ontario, to elect to receive a payment from the Estate equalizing the Net Family Property of one another;

(2) Under the Succession Law Reform Act, or any successor in the Province of Ontario, to share in the Estate of the other dying intestate or to an allowance or payment as a dependant from the Estate of the other;

(3) Under the Trustee Act or any successor in the Province of Ontario, to act as Executor or Administrator of the Will or the Estate of the other.

c) Financial Support:

Brown and Smith hereby forever release one another from any obligation to financially support one another.

d) Pension Rights:

Brown and Smith hereby agree that neither one of them will apply under the Canada Pension Plan for a division of pension credits accruing in favor of the other.

7. <u>GENERAL:</u>

a) Brown and Smith will each execute any document or documents reasonably required from time to time, to give effect to the terms and intent of this Agreement.

b) Brown and Smith each warrant that there are no representations, collateral agreements, or conditions affecting this Agreement, other than as expressed in this Agreement;

c) This Agreement may be amended or varied only by a further Instrument in writing, signed by Brown and Smith.

d) The provisions of this Agreement are binding on the respective heirs, executors, administrators, or assigns of Brown and Smith.

8. <u>PROPER LAW:</u>

The law governing the interpretation and implementation of this Agreement is the law prevailing from time to time in the Province of Ontario.

9. <u>MARRIAGE:</u>

If Brown and Smith should marry one another, this Agreement shall continue in force and shall be deemed to be a Marriage Contract under the Family Law Act.

10. <u>SEVERABILITY OF PROVISIONS:</u>

The invalidity or unenforceability of any provision of this Agreement will not affect the validity or enforceability of any other provision, and any invalid provision will be severable.

11. <u>INDEPENDENT LEGAL ADVICE:</u>

Brown and Smith each Acknowledge that he or she:

(a) has had independent Legal Advice;

(b) understands his or her rights and obligations under this Agreement;

(c) is signing this Agreement voluntarily; and

(d) has had complete financial disclosure of the assets and liabilities of one another.

TO EVIDENCE THEIR AGREEMENT, Brown and Smith have each signed this Agreement under seal.

SIGNED, SEALED, AND   )
DELIVERED   )
)
In the presence of:)
)
_J. M. Witness_____   )   _John Brown_____
WITNESS   )   JOHN BROWN
_Susie Dees_____   )   _Jane Smith_____
WITNESS   )   JANE SMITH

Many couples live together without getting married because they do not want the financial commitment that comes with marriage. However, unmarried spouses are entitled to financial support from their partners if they have been living together for a sufficient length of time (see chapter 7). If the spouses in a common-law relationship do not want this to happen, they would be wise to sign a cohabitation agreement that declares them financially independent of one another and releases them from all claims for financial support.

3. Separation agreements

A separation agreement (see Sample #3), may be entered into by married or unmarried spouses who are now living separate and apart. Many couples believe that they require a separation agreement to have a legal separation. As mentioned in chapter 2, this is not true. The separation is legal as soon as the spouses are living separate and apart with no intention of living together again. A separation agreement is useful, however, as proof of the date of separation.

The main purpose of a separation agreement is to settle the various issues between the spouses without going to court. In the agreement, the specific terms worked out on such issues as division of property, support, custody, and access are spelled out in writing. It is also customary to include a number of standard releases in a separation agreement (see Sample #3, clause 10). The releases ensure that neither spouse will apply to court to claim anything from the other that has not been dealt with in the agreement.

b. ARE DOMESTIC CONTRACTS ALWAYS BINDING?

The general rule is that a domestic contract is a legal document that can be enforced in court. But there are certain situations when a domestic contract, or part of it, can be set aside or disregarded by the court.

SAMPLE #3
SEPARATION AGREEMENT

THIS IS AN AGREEMENT made the 18th day of December, 199__,
BETWEEN:

SAM SMITH

— and —

SALLY SMITH

1. <u>BACKGROUND</u>:

(a) The parties were married to each other in the Town of Aurora, Ontario, on the 19th day of July, 1980. Throughout this Agreement, they are called, respectively, the "Husband" and the "Wife." If the marriage is dissolved, the first set of terms shall be construed to mean "former Husband" and "former Wife."

(b) The Husband and the Wife have two children, namely: Sue Smith, born January 31st, 1981, and Steve Smith, born April 3rd, 1983;

(c) The Husband and the Wife have been living separate and apart from each other since December 15th, 19__, and desire to settle by Agreement, all their rights and obligations which they have or may acquire with respect to their property, and maintenance or support from the other.

2. <u>AGREEMENT</u>:

The Husband and the Wife each agree to be bound by the provisions of this Agreement.

3. <u>LIVING SEPARATE AND APART</u>:

The Husband and the Wife will continue to live separate and apart from each other for the rest of their lives.

4. <u>FREEDOM FROM THE OTHER</u>:

Neither the Husband nor the Wife will molest, annoy, harass, or in any way interfere with the other, or attempt to compel the other to cohabit or live with him or her.

5. <u>SUPPORT AND MAINTENANCE</u>:

The Husband and the Wife each acknowledge that they are fully capable of supporting themselves now and in the future, and hereby forever release the other from any obligation to provide spousal support for one another.

6. <u>CUSTODY AND ACCESS</u>:

a) The Wife shall have custody of the children of the marriage, namely, Sue Smith, born January 31st, 1981, and Steve Smith, born April 3rd, 1983.

b) The Husband shall have reasonable access to the said children of the marriage, which access shall include the following visitation periods:

(i) The first and third Sunday of each month, from 10:00 a.m., until 6:00 p.m.;

(ii) Every other birthday, Christmas, and Easter;

24

    (iii)   A period of two weeks each summer, of which the Wife shall be given at least 30 days' notice.

7. CHILD SUPPORT:

Commencing November 1st, 19__, and on the 1st day of every month thereafter, the Husband shall pay the Wife child support in the amount of $200 per child, per month, which payments shall continue until the earliest of the following occur:

    (i)   The child reaches the age of 18 years, and ceases to attend a full-time educational institution;

    (ii)   The child reaches the age of 21 years;

    (iii)   The child ceases to reside full-time with the wife;

    (iv)   The child marries;

    (v)   The child dies.

8. VARIATION:

a) The parties intend Paragraphs 6 and 7 of this Agreement to be final, except for variation requested due to a material change in circumstances. In the event of a material change in circumstances, the party requesting the variation shall give the other party 30 days' notice of the variation sought, during which time the parties shall attempt to negotiate an amendment to this Agreement. If no agreement is reached during the said period, either party shall be at liberty to apply to Court to obtain the relief sought.

b) No provision of this Agreement other than Paragraphs 6 and 7, may be varied except by mutual written Agreement.

9. MATRIMONIAL HOME:

The Husband and the Wife acknowledge that the matrimonial home located at 111 San Santa, Apt. 3333, Downsview, Ontario, is rented accommodation. They agree in relation to the matrimonial home, that:

    (1)   The Wife shall be granted exclusive possession of the matrimonial home and its contents.

10. RELEASES:

Property: Except as provided in this Agreement, the Husband and the Wife each acknowledge and agree, that:

(a) all their property has been divided between them to their mutual satisfaction;

(b) each is entitled to property now in his or her possession, free of any claim from the other;

(c) each may dispose of the property they now possess as if they were unmarried;

(d) each releases and discharges all rights to and interests in property owned by the other that he or she has or may during his or her lifetime acquire under the laws of any jurisdiction, and in particular the Family Law Act, R.S.O. 1990, or any successor in the Province of Ontario, including all rights to and interest in:

   (i)   Ownership in property;

   (ii)   Division of property;

   (iii) Compensation by payment of an amount of money, or by an award of a share of property for contribution of any kind, whether direct or indirect, made to property;

   (iv) A payment for the purpose of equalizing Net Family Property of the Husband and the Wife.

(e) This section is a complete defence to any action brought by either the Husband or the Wife to assert a claim to any property, wherever situate, in which the other has or had an interest.

(f) Each releases any rights they have as beneficiary under an insurance policy on the life or person of the other.

Debts and Obligations:

(a) Neither the Husband nor the Wife will contract in the name of the other, or bind the other in any way for any debts or obligations;

(b) If debts or obligations are incurred by the Husband or the Wife on behalf of the other, before or after the date of this Agreement, he or she will indemnify the other from all costs, expenses, damages, and actions arising from those debts or obligations.

Release of Rights to Estate:

Except as provided in this Agreement, and subject to any right given by the other in his or her Will, the Husband and the Wife each release and discharge all rights that he or she has or may have under the laws of any jurisdiction in the Estate of the other and in particular:

(a) Under the Succession Law Reform Act, R.S.O. 1990, or any successor in the Province of Ontario,

   (i)   to share in the Estate of the other upon the other dying intestate, or;

   (ii)   to an allowance or payment as a dependant from the Estate of the other;

(b) Under the Trustee Act or any successor in the Province of Ontario to act as Executor or Administrator of the Will or the Estate of the other; and

(c) Under the Family Law Act, R.S.O. 1990, to elect to receive a payment from the Estate for the purpose of equalizing the Net Family property of the Husband and the Wife.

General:

(a) The Husband and the Wife each accept the provisions of this Agreement in satisfaction of all claims and causes of action each now has, including, but not limited to claims and causes of action for maintenance, support, interim maintenance or interim support, possession of or title to property, entitlement to an equal share of Net Family Property, or any other claim arising out of the marriage of the Husband or the Wife, EXCEPT for claims and causes of action:

(i) arising under this Agreement;

(ii) for a Decree of Divorce.

(b) Nothing in this Agreement will bar any action or proceeding by either the Husband or the Wife to enforce any of the terms of this Agreement.

11. SEPARATION AGREEMENT TO SURVIVE DIVORCE:

If either the Husband or the Wife obtains a Decree of Divorce, all the terms of this Agreement will survive and continue in force.

12. NINETY-DAY TRIAL COHABITATION

If at any future time, the Husband and the Wife, with their mutual consent, cohabit as Husband and Wife for a period or periods totalling not more than 90 days with reconciliation as the primary purpose of the cohabitation, the provisions contained in this Agreement will not be affected, except as provided in this clause. If the Husband and the Wife with their mutual consent cohabit as Husband and Wife for a period or periods totalling more than 90 days, with reconciliation as the primary purpose of the cohabitation, the provisions contained in this Agreement will become void, except that nothing in this Paragraph will affect or invalidate any payment, conveyance, or act made or done pursuant to the provisions of this Agreement.

13. GENERAL

(a) The Husband and Wife will each execute any document or documents reasonably required from time to time, to give effect to the terms and intent of this Agreement;

(b) The Husband and Wife each warrant that there are no representations, collateral agreements, or conditions affecting this Agreement, other than as expressed in this Agreement;

(c) Subject to Paragraph 8 hereof, this Agreement may be amended only by a further instrument in writing, signed by the Husband and by the Wife;

(d) The provisions of this Agreement are binding on the respective heirs, executors, administrators, or assigns of the Husband and the Wife;

(e) Neither the Husband nor the Wife will apply under the Canada Pension Plan for a division of pension credits after the dissolution of their marriage.

14. <u>PROPER LAW:</u>

The law governing the interpretation and implementation of this Agreement is the law prevailing from time to time in the Province of Ontario.

15. <u>SEVERABILITY OF PROVISIONS:</u>

The invalidity or unenforceability of any provision of this Agreement will not affect the validity or enforceability of any other provision, and any invalid provision will be severable.

16. <u>INDEPENDENT LEGAL ADVICE AND FINANCIAL DISCLOSURE:</u>

The Husband and the Wife each acknowledge that he or she:

(a) has had independent legal advice;

(b) understands his or her respective rights and obligations under this Agreement;

(c) is signing this Agreement voluntarily; and

(d) has had full financial disclosure of the assets and liabilities of one another.

TO EVIDENCE THEIR AGREEMENT, the Husband and the Wife have each signed this Agreement under seal.

SIGNED, SEALED, AND	)
DELIVERED	)
	)
In the presence of:	)
	)
Jane Bloch	) *Sam Smith*
Witness as to Husband	) SAM SMITH
Frank Jones	) *Sally Smith*
Witness as to Wife	) SALLY SMITH

1. Contracts affecting children

Although a marriage contract cannot deal with custody and access to children, a separation agreement can and usually does deal with these matters, as well as the question of child support. However, since the child is not a party to the contract, the court will not permit the parents to bargain away the rights of the child. Accordingly, the court may disregard any provision of a domestic contract concerning a child if the court decides it is in the best interests of that child to do so.

2. The matrimonial home

A marriage contract limiting a spouse's right to live in the matrimonial home or removing the requirement to obtain consent to a sale of the house is not enforceable. However, these provisions are enforceable in a separation agreement. In fact, it is quite common for a separation agreement to provide one spouse with exclusive possession of the matrimonial home.

3. Support provisions

The court may overturn a provision for support in a domestic contract if it results in circumstances that are unconscionable. For example, a person in need of support may have agreed to little or no spousal support because the other spouse was in a low-paying job and was not able to make payments. If the other spouse later won a lottery and became a millionaire, it would be unreasonable to uphold the waiver of support and the court would likely disregard it.

The court can also disregard a support provision or a waiver of support for a spouse who will have to be supported by welfare or other public money. Finally, if a spouse defaults in paying the support set out in the domestic contract, the support provision may be set aside, and an application for support may be made (see chapter 7).

4.   Non-disclosure

Before signing a domestic contract, you and your spouse are legally required to disclose your significant assets and debts to one another. This is to ensure that each spouse can make an informed decision about agreeing to the contract. For example, a woman who believed that her husband's only assets were a car and his personal belongings would be very likely to release all property claims in a separation agreement. However, if she knew that her husband had acquired $100 000 worth of shares in his employer's company through an employee stock option plan, her position would be quite different. Any domestic contract signed without financial disclosure can be disregarded by the court.

5.   Understanding the contract

Most people are aware that they should never sign anything without reading and understanding it. Nevertheless, many lengthy documents are signed this way, either from lack of time or too great a trust in the preparer of the document. If a problem surfaces later, the person says, "I didn't know I signed anything like that." If this happens with a domestic contract, the court has the power to set aside all or part of the contract. However, the court may not exercise this power. The court will not have much sympathy for a person who signs a document blindly and then applies to the court for help.

It is customary for each party to a domestic contract to review the document with his or her own lawyer before signing it. The lawyer then completes a form known as a certificate of independent legal advice that is then attached to the contract (see Sample #4). Once this is done, it is very difficult for a party to the contract to claim later that he or she did not understand it.

6.   Dum casta clause

Many years ago, it was common for a separation agreement to state that a woman would only receive support so long as

SAMPLE #4
CERTIFICATE OF INDEPENDENT LEGAL ADVICE

I, Larry Lawyer, of the City of North York, in the Municipality of Metropolitan Toronto, Barrister and Solicitor, DO HEREBY CERTIFY that I was this day consulted in my professional capacity by John Doe, named in the annexed Marriage Contract, dated the 20th day of October, 199_, as to his obligations and rights under the said Agreement, that I acted solely for him and explained fully to him the nature and effect of the said Agreement, and he did acknowledge and declare that he fully understood the nature and effect thereof and did execute the said document in my presence and did acknowledge and declare, and it appeared to me, that he was executing the said document of his own volition and without fear, threats, compulsion, or influence by Jane Doe, or any other person.

DATED this 29th day of October, 199_.

Larry Lawyer

she remained chaste. This type of clause is clearly objectionable and is no longer enforceable. However, it is still valid to include a clause saying that support payments may cease upon a spouse's remarriage or cohabitation with another person.

7. Barriers to remarriage

In the Jewish and Islamic faiths, a woman cannot remarry within her faith until she receives a religious bill of divorce from her husband. An unscrupulous husband may take advantage of this by threatening to withhold the religious divorce unless his wife agrees to a favorable financial settlement. If the wife can prove that she signed a separation agreement under a threat of this nature, she may apply to court to have all or part of the agreement overturned.

c. CAN A DOMESTIC CONTRACT BE VARIED?

A domestic contract is intended to be a final resolution of the affairs of the parties. There is no automatic right to have it varied, even if the circumstances of the spouses have substantially changed. Therefore, many agreements contain a special clause stating that the contract may be varied if there is a material change in circumstances (for example, if one spouse became physically disabled). If those circumstances happen and the parties cannot agree on the variation, either one may apply to court to decide the matter.

If your separation agreement does not provide a right of variation, don't despair. There is a possibility that the clause you wish to vary may be invalid on one of the grounds described in section **b.** above. You should consult a lawyer to determine whether this is the case.

d. DO I NEED A LAWYER TO PREPARE THE DOMESTIC CONTRACT?

You can draw up your domestic contract yourself, using the sample contracts in this chapter as a guide in deciding what you want to include in your own contract.

Even if you decide to have a lawyer draft the contract for you, the substantial terms of the agreement are for you and your spouse to decide. Many people go to their lawyer for a domestic contract without any idea of what it should contain or what terms are agreeable to them. This situation is frustrating for the lawyer and costly for the client because a great deal of time must be spent negotiating the terms of the agreement — negotiation that you and your spouse could do yourselves.

After reading this book, you and your spouse will be well informed and in a good position to negotiate your own agreement. The agreement can then be prepared by your lawyer at a relatively low cost, or you may use one of the packages of forms.

If you prepare the agreement yourself, you may still find it useful to consult a lawyer to ensure that the contract is in clear, legally enforceable language. You should also have different lawyers review the contract for each of you so you can each attach a certificate of independent legal advice to it.

4

DIVORCE AND ANNULMENT

a. DO I NEED A DIVORCE?

In the eyes of the law, the main reason that you need a divorce is to permit you to marry someone else. Your rights to division of property, support, custody, and access are available on separation whether or not you are divorced. Nevertheless, many people who separate want a divorce as soon as possible for religious or moral reasons, or simply to sever the psychological ties with their spouse.

It is important for spouses to think very carefully and perhaps seek counselling before beginning divorce proceedings. In fact, every lawyer who acts on behalf of a spouse in a divorce proceeding is obliged by law to discuss the possibility of reconciliation with his or her client. The lawyer is also required to provide the client with the addresses of counselling and mediation centres that might be able to assist the spouses to achieve a reconciliation. (See chapter 9 for more information on mediation.)

b. WHAT ARE THE GROUNDS FOR DIVORCE?

You are not entitled to a divorce simply because you and your spouse consent to it. You must establish grounds for divorce. Under the Divorce Act, there is one ground for divorce: marriage breakdown. However, that ground can be established in one of three ways: separation, adultery, or cruelty.

1. Separation

The most common basis for divorce is separation. The spouses must be living separate and apart when the divorce proceeding is started and must remain separated for at least one year before the divorce order is granted. In other words, you may begin the divorce proceeding as soon as you are separated as long as the separation has lasted for a year or longer by the time the case is heard by the court.

Usually the period of separation begins on the date that one of the spouses moves out of the matrimonial home and does not return. However, there have been cases where a court has granted a divorce to two people who are living separate and apart under the same roof. Although the couple still reside in the same house (usually for economic reasons), they are considered separated if their social, sexual, and financial lives are completely unrelated and distinct from one another. Under these circumstances, either spouse may petition for a divorce on the grounds of separation.

Couples who have separated and later attempt a reconciliation may resume cohabitation for up to 90 days without interrupting the period of separation needed to establish grounds for divorce. If the period or periods of cohabitation total more than 90 days, the spouses are considered to be reconciled, in which case the earlier period of separation is no longer valid as a ground for divorce.

2. Adultery

Either spouse may petition for divorce on the basis that the other spouse has committed adultery, which is an act of sexual intercourse with a person other than one's spouse. If adultery is established, a divorce can be obtained without meeting the requirement of a one-year separation.

The difficulty with adultery is that you must prove it in court with proper evidence before it will be accepted. Unless you are prepared to hire a private detective to obtain proof of adultery, the only practical way to establish it is by having your spouse admit that he or she committed adultery. You need your spouse's co-operation to do this, because the Ontario Evidence Act permits a spouse to refuse to answer any question that would indicate he or she has committed adultery. However, adultery no longer carries the stigma it once did, and many spouses are willing to admit to adultery in order to hasten the divorce.

3. Cruelty

The third basis for divorce is physical or mental cruelty that makes the continued cohabitation of the spouses intolerable. This is the most distasteful way of obtaining a divorce, as it requires the petitioner (the spouse applying for the divorce) to recount all the nasty things his or her spouse has done and the effect that this conduct has had on the marriage. It is also necessary to prove the acts of cruelty, either by the evidence of independent witnesses or by medical or police reports.

It often happens that the spouse being accused of cruelty responds with a similar description of the cruel conduct of the petitioner. These divorce contests are emotionally and often financially exhausting. Most spouses are better off waiting for a divorce based on a one-year separation rather than resorting to establishing cruelty.

c. CAN THE COURT REFUSE TO GRANT A DIVORCE?

Once the grounds for divorce outlined above are demonstrated, the court almost always grants a divorce order. However, the court has the power, under certain circumstances, to refuse to grant a divorce, although this power is rarely exercised. These circumstances are known as bars to divorce and are briefly described below.

1. Collusion

Collusion includes any agreement to fabricate or suppress evidence to deceive the court. The most obvious example of collusion is lying to the court about the period of separation or about the commission of adultery. An interesting example of collusion occurs when a Canadian citizen marries someone from another country solely for the purpose of sponsoring that person's immigration and seeks a divorce as soon as the immigration is completed. Courts have dismissed such applications because the parties were guilty of collusion.

2. Condonation or connivance

Condonation means that the petitioning spouse has in effect forgiven the cruel or adulterous conduct of the other spouse by taking him or her back. It is usually considered condonation if the parties have continued to cohabit for more than 90 days since the cruelty or adultery took place.

Connivance means that the spouse petitioning for divorce has encouraged the other spouse to commit acts of cruelty or adultery in order to establish grounds for divorce. Although it rarely occurs, a court does have the power to refuse a divorce on this basis.

3. Support of children

If there are children of the marriage, the court must be satisfied that reasonable arrangements have been made for their support before a divorce will be granted. Paragraph 27 of the Petition for Divorce (see Sample #5) asks you to set out the details of the child support that have been made. If no child support is being paid, and you have not requested child support in the petition, the court may refuse to grant the divorce unless a satisfactory explanation is given for the absence of child support. The most common explanation is that the father is on public assistance and has no income with which to pay child support.

SAMPLE #5
PETITION FOR DIVORCE

Court file no._____

ONTARIO COURT (GENERAL DIVISION)

BETWEEN:

(Court seal)

Joan Public   **PETITIONER**

(wife   )

and

John Que Public   **RESPONDENT**

(husband   )

PETITION FOR DIVORCE

TO THE RESPONDENT

A LEGAL PROCEEDING FOR DIVORCE HAS BEEN COMMENCED AGAINST YOU by the petitioner. The claim made against you appears on the following pages.

IF YOU WISH TO DEFEND THIS PROCEEDING, you or an Ontario lawyer acting for you must prepare an answer in Form 69D prescribed by the Rules of Civil Procedure, serve it on the petitioner's lawyer(s) or, where the petitioner does not have a lawyer, serve it on the petitioner, and file it, with proof of service, in this court office, WITHIN TWENTY DAYS after this petition is served on you, if you are served in Ontario.

If you are served in another province or territory of Canada or in the United States of America, the period for serving and filing your answer is forty days. If you are served outside Canada and the United States of America, the period is sixty days.

Instead of serving and filing an answer, you may serve and file a notice of intent to defend in Form 69J prescribed by the Rules of Civil Procedure. This will entitle you to ten more days within which to serve and file your answer.

If this petition for divorce contains a claim for support or division of property, you must serve and file a financial statement in Form 69K prescribed by the Rules of Civil Procedure within the time set out above for serving and filing your answer, whether or not you wish to defend this proceeding. If you serve and file an answer, your financial statement must accompany your answer.

IF YOU FAIL TO SERVE AND FILE AN ANSWER, A DIVORCE MAY BE GRANTED IN YOUR ABSENCE AND WITHOUT FURTHER NOTICE TO YOU, JUDGMENT MAY BE GRANTED AGAINST YOU ON ANY OTHER CLAIM IN THIS PETITION AND YOU MAY LOSE YOUR RIGHT TO SUPPORT OR DIVISION OF PROPERTY. IF YOU WISH TO DEFEND THIS PROCEEDING BUT ARE UNABLE TO PAY LEGAL FEES, LEGAL AID MAY BE AVAILABLE TO YOU BY CONTACTING A LOCAL LEGAL AID OFFICE.

NEITHER SPOUSE IS FREE TO REMARRY until a divorce has been granted and has taken effect. Once a divorce has taken effect, you may obtain a certificate of divorce from this court office.

Date _____ Issued by_____

Local registrar

To: John Que Public
1000 Yonge Street
Toronto, Ontario
Z1P 0G0

Address of court office

145 Queen Street West
Toronto, Ontario
Z1P 0G0

SAMPLE #5 — Continued

CLAIM

1. The petitioner claims:

    (a)   a divorce;

    (b)   under the *Divorce Act*,

        (i)

    (c)   under the *Family Law Act*,

        (i)

GROUNDS FOR DIVORCE — SEPARATION

2. (a) The spouses have lived separate and apart since <u>June 1, 19</u> ___ . The spouses have
resumed cohabitation during the following periods in an unsuccessful attempt at reconciliation:
Date(s) of cohabitation
(If none, state "none.")

None

GROUNDS FOR DIVORCE — ADULTERY

2. (b) ~~The respondent spouse has committed adultery. Particulars are as follows:~~

GROUNDS FOR DIVORCE — CRUELTY

2. (c) ~~The respondent has treated the petitioner with physical or mental cruelty of such a kind as to
render intolerable the continued cohabitation of the spouses. Particulars are as follows:~~

SAMPLE #5 — Continued

RECONCILIATION

3. There is no possibility of reconciliation of the spouses.

4. The following efforts to reconcile have been made:

None

DETAILS OF MARRIAGE

5. Date of marriage: _____December 17, 1984_____

6. Place of marriage: _____Toronto, Ontario_____
   (municipality and province, state, or country)

7. Wife's surname immediately before marriage: _____Jones_____

8. Wife's surname at birth: _____Jones_____

9. Husband's surname immediately before marriage: _____Que Public_____

10. Husband's surname at birth: _____Que Public_____

11. Marital status of husband at time of marriage: _____Never married_____
    (never married, divorced, or widower)

12. Marital status of wife at time of marriage: _____Never married_____
    (never married, divorced, or widow)

13. Wife's birthplace: _____Toronto, Ontario_____
    (province, state, or country)

14. Wife's birth date: _____April 11, 1945_____

15. Husband's birthplace: _____Calgary, Alberta_____
    (province, state, or country)

16. Husband's birth date: _____May 12, 1944_____

(Check (a), (b) or (c)
and complete as
required.)

17. (a) ☐ A certificate of ☐ the marriage
        ☒ the registration of the marriage

    of the spouses has been filed with the court.

    (b) ☐ ~~It is impossible to obtain a certificate of the marriage or its registration because:~~

    (c) ☐ ~~A certificate of the marriage or its registration will be filed before this action is set down~~
        ~~for trial or a motion is made for judgment.~~

41

RESIDENCE

18. The petitioner has resided in: ___Toronto, Ontario___
(municipality and province, state, or country)

since ___birth___
(date)

19. The respondent has resided in: ___Toronto, Ontario___
(municipality and province, state, or country)

since ___December, 1982___
(date)

20. The respondent's current address is: ___1000 Yonge Street, Toronto, Ontario___

21. The ☒ petitioner has habitually resided in Ontario for at least one year immediately preceding the
    ☐ respondent

commencement of this proceeding.

CHILDREN

22. The following are all living children of the marriage as defined by the *Divorce Act:*

Full name	Birth date	School and grade or year	Person with whom child lives and length of time child has lived there

There are no children of the marriage

The children ordinarily reside in: _____
(municipality and province, state, or country)

23. (a) The petitioner seeks an order for custody or joint custody of the following children on the following terms:

Name of child	Terms of the order

Not applicable

The respondent ☐ agrees
            ☐ does not agree with the above terms.

(b) ~~The petitioner is not seeking an order for custody and~~

☐ is content that a previous order for custody remain in force

☐ is attempting to obtain an order for custody in another proceeding

full particulars of which are as follows:

(c) ~~The petitioner seeks an order for access (visiting arrangements) and is content that the respondent have an order for custody of the following children on the following terms:~~

Name of child	Terms of the order

☐ agrees
The respondent ☐ does not agree with the above terms.

24. (a) The following are the existing visiting arrangements (access) for the spouse who does not have the children living with him or her:

Not applicable

(b) The existing arrangements (access) are ☐ satisfactory
☐ not satisfactory.

Not applicable

25. The order sought in paragraph 23 is in the best interests of the children for the following reasons:

Not applicable

26. The following material changes in the circumstances of the spouses are expected to affect the children, their custody and the visiting arrangements (access) in the future:

Not applicable

27. (a) The existing arrangements between the spouses for support for the children are as follows:

Amount paid	Time period (weekly, monthly, etc.)	Paid by (husband or wife)	Paid for (name of child)

Not applicable

(b) The existing support arrangements ☐ are being honoured
☐ are not being honoured.

Not applicable

(c) The petitioner proposes that the support arrangements for the children should be as follows:

Amount paid	Time period (weekly, monthly, etc.)	To be paid by (husband or wife)	To be paid for (name of child)

Not applicable

28. The educational needs of the children ☐ are being met
☐ are not being met.

Not applicable

OTHER COURT PROCEEDINGS

29. The following are all other court proceedings with reference to the marriage or any child of the marriage.

Not applicable

DOMESTIC CONTRACTS AND FINANCIAL ARRANGEMENTS

30. The spouses have entered into the following domestic contracts and other written or oral financial arrangements:

Date	Nature of contract or arrangement	Status

There are no domestic contracts of other written or oral financial arrangements between the Husband and the Wife.

COLLUSION, CONDONATION, AND CONNIVANCE

31. There has been no collusion in relation to this divorce proceeding.

32. ~~There has been no condonation of or connivance at the grounds for divorce in this proceeding.~~

SAMPLE #5 — Continued

MATTERS OTHER THAN DIVORCE AND CUSTODY

33.   The grounds for the relief sought in paragraph 1, other than a divorce or custody, are as follows:

Not applicable.

SAMPLE #5 — Continued

TRIAL

Where a claim is made for custody of a child who ordinarily resides in Ontario, the place of trial must be in the county where he or she ordinarily resides.

34. The petitioner proposes that if there is a trial in this action, it be held at:
    Toronto, Ontario

DECLARATION OF PETITIONER

35. I have read and understand this petition for divorce. The statements in it are true, to the best of my knowledge, information, and belief.

Date_____ May 2, 199-_____   _____ *Joan Public* _____
                                          (Signature of petitioner)

(Name, address, and telephone number of petitioner)

Joan Public
322 Lakeshore Road
Toronto Ontario Z1P 0G0
(101) 123-4567

INTERNATIONAL SELF-COUNSEL PRESS LTD.
1481 Charlotte Road
North Vancouver, B.C. V7J 1H1
DIVORT-SOLE(1-12) 91

4. Barriers to remarriage

As mentioned in chapter 3, certain cultures require the husband to deliver to his wife a religious bill of divorce before she is permitted to re-marry within her faith. As a result, there have been cases where the husband has used the delivery of a religious divorce as a bargaining tool to obtain a favorable settlement in the divorce proceeding. The Divorce Act gives the court the power to withhold the granting of a divorce or other relief to a spouse who refuses to remove barriers to the religious re-marriage of the other spouse. The court can also strike out any defence or counter-petition filed by the refusing spouse. The amendment is designed to discourage the use of unfair pressure to obtain an advantage in divorce proceedings.

d. DO I NEED MY SPOUSE'S CONSENT TO GET A DIVORCE?

It is not necessary to obtain your spouse's consent to the divorce petition. If the court is satisfied that there are grounds for divorce and none of the bars to divorce applies, it will order the divorce even if your spouse does not consent. However, your spouse must be served with the divorce petition and given an opportunity to answer all or part of it. If no answer is made within the prescribed time, the divorce becomes an uncontested divorce and will usually be completed fairly quickly.

If you do not know where your spouse is, you must apply to court to obtain an order for service of the divorce petition by a different method (for example, by mail to your spouse's last known address or by advertisement in the newspaper). If appropriate, the court may dispense with service of the petition altogether.

e. CAN WE SUE FOR DIVORCE TOGETHER?

Under the Divorce Act, a husband and wife can jointly petition for divorce, but only on the basis of a one-year separation and only if nothing is asked for but the divorce. If one of the parties wishes custody or maintenance, a joint petition is not permitted unless those orders are consented to by the other spouse. Once the petition is filed, it need not be served. You should ensure that you have independent legal advice prior to commencing a petition for divorce or filing an answer. It is a very important legal document and you may have rights you are unaware of and that should be claimed in a petition for divorce.

f. DO I NEED TO APPEAR IN COURT FOR MY DIVORCE?

If the divorce petition is uncontested, it is not necessary for you to appear in court to obtain the divorce. You can present your evidence to the court in a sworn affidavit that is filed with the court and taken to a judge who reads it together with the petition for divorce. If satisfied with the affidavit evidence, the judge will issue the divorce order.

g. WHICH COURT HAS THE POWER TO GRANT MY DIVORCE?

In the province of Ontario, only the Ontario Court (General Division) has jurisdiction to hear divorce cases. The divorce application may be made in Ontario as long as either spouse has been ordinarily resident in Ontario for at least one year immediately prior to the application.

If the spouses live in two different provinces and they each bring a divorce petition in their own province, the petition brought first is entitled to proceed and the second one is deemed to be discontinued. If both petitions were brought on the same day and neither one is discontinued, then the Trial Division of the Federal Court has exclusive jurisdiction to hear the divorce.

h. PROCEDURE OF AN UNCONTESTED DIVORCE

Following are the usual steps involved in a simple uncontested divorce in Ontario. Remember that each case is slightly different and that there may be variations in the procedure to meet the needs of a particular situation. This is a brief summary for information purposes only. If you wish detailed information for handling your own divorce, see the *Divorce Guide for Ontario*, another title in the Self-Counsel Series.

(a) Complete three copies of the petition for divorce. This prescribed form deals with the grounds for divorce, the possibility of reconciliation, the details of the marriage, and any claims for custody, support, or division of property. The petition for divorce should be completed as carefully and completely as possible, as it forms the basis for the divorce judgment granted by the Court. A completed divorce petition is shown in Sample #5.

(b) Take the divorce petition and your marriage certificate to the office of the Ontario Court (General Division) in your region. In Metropolitan Toronto, the Court is located at 145 Queen Street West, Toronto. If you do not have a marriage certificate, you should obtain one by writing to the appropriate office in the province or country where you were married. If you were married in Ontario, you can obtain a marriage certificate from the Registrar General.

(c) A clerk in the Court office will review the petition and correct any errors or omissions in it. When you pay the prescribed fee, the clerk will issue the petition by signing it and placing the Court seal on it. The clerk will return the original petition to you and keep a copy for the Court file.

(d) Once the petition is issued, a copy of it must be personally served on your spouse by someone other than yourself. This can be done through the sheriff's office of the county or district in which your spouse lives. There are also a number of private process servers who will do the job faster than the sheriff's office. If your spouse is easily located, the average cost of service is about $50. Once the petition is served, the process server must complete an affidavit of service stating the date of service and the method of service.

(e) After the petition is served, you must wait 20 days from the date of service (longer if your spouse lives outside Ontario), during which time your spouse (known as the respondent) may contest the divorce by serving and filing an answer. If your spouse does not file an answer, the divorce is uncontested.

Note: If you and your spouse are completing a joint petition for divorce (see section **e.** above) both of you sign the petition and the 20-day waiting period is not required.

(f) The next step is to bring a motion for judgment for divorce and any other relief (that is, a claim for support, division of property, custody, or access) requested in the petition.

You do this by going once again to the Ontario Court office with four documents: the original petition for divorce and proof of service, a motion for judgment, a supporting affidavit or affidavits, and three unsigned copies of the judgment for divorce. The motion for judgment is a standard form document stating that a divorce (and other relief) is being claimed and listing the affidavits on which the claim is based.

The supporting affidavit that you file confirms that the information contained in the petition for divorce is true and sets out the grounds for the divorce and any other relief claimed. It is usual for a second affidavit to be filed (by your spouse or a third party) confirming the information in your affidavit. For examples of the supporting affidavit and the judgment for divorce, see the *Divorce Guide for Ontario*.

(g) The motion for judgment is combined with a copy of the petition for divorce and the supporting affidavit to form a booklet known as a motion record.

If your motion record is in order and a judge is satisfied that you are entitled to the relief claimed, the judgment for divorce will be signed, sealed, and mailed back to you and your spouse. (You should provide two pre-addressed stamped envelopes for this purpose.) If the judge requires additional evidence, or if the judgment you prepared needs to be changed, the judgment will not be signed and you should contact the Court office to find out what is required.

i. WHEN DOES THE DIVORCE BECOME FINAL?

After the divorce is granted, there is a 30-day waiting period. If no appeal is filed during that time, the divorce becomes final on the 31st day following the grant of divorce.

If the 30-day waiting period is a serious inconvenience to one of the parties, the Court has the power to dispense with it if both parties agree not to appeal the divorce judgment. For example, the waiting period may be dispensed with in the case of a woman who is nine months pregnant with another man's child and wants to marry him before the baby is born.

Once the divorce becomes final and the registrar of the Court is satisfied that no appeal is pending, you may obtain a certificate of divorce from the Court office.

j. WHAT IF I AM SERVED WITH DIVORCE PAPERS?

If you are served with a petition for divorce, do not ignore it, but do not call a lawyer immediately. You can do several things before you decide whether you need a lawyer.

First, read all of the papers carefully and note any statements or claims that you disagree with. Pay particular attention to the paragraph that lists the items claimed by your spouse (the petitioner). If the only claim is for a divorce (and possible legal costs) and you do not want to make a counterclaim, you should probably not contest the divorce. Since your marriage has broken down, the divorce will benefit both you and your spouse, and the legal process will be quicker and less costly if you do not contest it. Even if you want to contest the divorce, there is no legal basis to do so if your marriage has broken down and you have been separated for a year or more.

If your only objection to the divorce is the claim for legal costs, contact the solicitor who prepared the application. He or she may be willing to waive or reduce the claim for costs in exchange for your agreement not to contest the divorce.

The situation is more complicated if —

(a) the divorce includes a claim for support, custody, or access (called corollary relief),

(b) there is an application under the Family Law Act for division of property included in the divorce petition, or

(c) you wish to counterclaim for any of these items.

If any of the above situations apply to you, you should almost certainly consult a lawyer and discuss the petition and your position with him or her.

If you and your spouse can agree on all or most of the items, it should be possible to settle the matter by written agreement and allow the divorce to proceed on an uncontested basis. The savings in time, legal fees, and aggravation will be a great advantage. However, if you are unable to reach a quick agreement, you or your lawyer must contest the application by filing a written answer and/or counterpetition and completing a financial statement. Financial statements are discussed in more detail in chapter 6.

k. DO I NEED A LAWYER FOR MY DIVORCE?

An application for a simple uncontested divorce is not difficult, and you should be able to carry it out yourself. Read through the divorce procedure described earlier for an overview of the process. You also need a copy of the *Divorce Guide for Ontario* and the accompanying package of forms, both published by Self-Counsel Press. The book and kit will provide the instructions and the forms you need to complete your divorce.

Pay close attention to the instructions given by Court staff when you file your forms. The staff are normally helpful in answering your questions, however, they do not have the time to guide you step by step through the process. If you are having difficulty completing the petition, or if you get stuck on technical court procedures, you can always consult a lawyer on a periodic basis for temporary assistance. This costs less than having a lawyer represent you throughout and it is probably all the help you need.

If the divorce is contested, you would be wise to retain a competent family law lawyer to represent you. A contested divorce is like any other lawsuit, and you should not attempt to handle it yourself. Choosing a lawyer is discussed in more detail in chapter 9.

l. ANNULMENT OF A MARRIAGE

1. The difference between divorce and annulment

An annulment is not the same as a divorce. An annulment is a declaration that the marriage is not valid and the partners are not legally married. A divorce is the dissolution of a marriage that was legal and officially valid. A divorce is easier to obtain than an annulment; usually you are far better off proceeding by petition for divorce. However, there are cases where a court will refuse to grant a divorce because the validity of the marriage itself is in question. In these circumstances, the only alternative is an annulment.

2. The grounds for annulment

All the grounds for annulment are in some way related to a deficiency in the marriage or the marriage partners. The most common ground is the existence of a prior valid marriage, which makes the subsequent marriage illegal and void. Marriages between parties who are under age, or mentally incapable of understanding the marriage ceremony, or related in a forbidden blood relationship (see Table #1) are also subject to annulment. Another ground for annulment is lack of consent by one of the parties to the marriage. This can occur where the marriage is performed under duress, fear, or fraud.

Some courts have also held that when an immigrant marries a Canadian solely for the purpose of getting into Canada, there is no true intent to marry and the marriage can be annulled.

The final ground for annulment is incapacity to consummate the marriage. If one of the parties suffers from an incurable inability to have sexual intercourse following the marriage, the marriage may be annulled at the request of the other party.

3. What about other claims following annulment?

The Divorce Act does not apply to marriages that are annulled (because no divorce has taken place; the marriage has simply been declared void). Accordingly, the spouses may not claim support, custody, or access under the Divorce Act following an annulment. However, rights under provincial legislation continue to apply to a spouse who entered into a marriage that is void as long as he or she did so in good faith. That spouse may apply under such legislation for division of property, support, custody, and access (see chapters 6, 7, and 8).

5

THE MATRIMONIAL HOME

The matrimonial home is in a special category as far as the property of the marriage is concerned. Because the issue of where the spouses are to live is usually of immediate concern, this chapter discusses the special rights attached to the matrimonial home. The division of the matrimonial home and other family property is discussed in chapter 6.

a. WHAT IS THE MATRIMONIAL HOME?

To qualify as a matrimonial home, your property must be ordinarily occupied by you and your spouse as a family residence, and it must be owned or leased by one or both of you. If you and your spouse are separated, the matrimonial home is the property that was ordinarily occupied by you and your spouse at the time of separation.

If you own and occupy more than one property, such as a city home and a country cottage, both properties are considered matrimonial homes unless you complete and register a designation naming only one property as your matrimonial home.

b. POSSESSION OF A MATRIMONIAL HOME

1. The equal right of possession

Both spouses have an equal right of possession of the matrimonial home. This means that regardless of who owns the home each spouse is entitled to live in it. If the spouse who owns the matrimonial home dies, the surviving spouse is entitled to continue living in the home rent-free for up to 60 days following the date of death.

2. How can I get my spouse out of the house?

In many family disputes, the relationship between the spouses has broken down, yet neither spouse is willing to leave the house. For example, consider the case of a wife who discovers that her husband is having an affair. The wife is furious and wants to leave her husband's things in the driveway and change the locks on their jointly owned home. But can she do this? Unless the wife obtains a court order for exclusive possession of the home, the answer is clearly no.

3. What is an order for exclusive possession?

Regardless of who owns the matrimonial home, either spouse can apply to court at any time during the marriage for an order of exclusive possession of the home. The effect of this order is to exclude one of the spouses from entering the home. If the excluded spouse is still living in the home, the order will require him or her to leave immediately. The order can also direct that all or part of the household furnishings remain in the home, and it can require the excluded spouse to pay the costs of maintenance and the mortgage.

4. How can I get an order for exclusive possession?

An order for exclusive possession is a very severe remedy, as it basically deprives one spouse of the right to enjoy his or her own property. It follows that the order will only be made in limited circumstances.

In the example given above, if the couple have no children living in the house and they are both employed, the court would probably refuse the order. That the husband has been unfaithful is not a sufficient reason to deprive him of the benefit of his property. Moreover, the wife is working and is financially capable of living elsewhere. A more appropriate order would be that the house be sold and the net proceeds divided between the parties.

On the other hand, suppose the wife is not employed and is caring for the couple's three young children. In that instance, a sale of the house may not be a good idea for two reasons. First, it would be disruptive and detrimental to the best interests of the children to move to other, probably smaller accommodations. Second, since the wife does not earn income, she would not be able to pay for other accommodations, particularly if she retained custody of the children.

In such a situation, the court would be likely to order exclusive possession in favor of the wife, as long as the husband was already living elsewhere. If the husband was still living in the home, the court might order him to leave if there was evidence that his presence in the home was bad for the children or that he had committed acts of violence against his wife or children.

5. How is an order for exclusive possession enforced?

A spouse who violates an order for exclusive possession is guilty of a criminal offence. A police officer may arrest the spouse without warrant; if convicted, the spouse is liable to a fine or imprisonment.

6. Is an order for exclusive possession permanent?

The order for exclusive possession may be permanent or for any period that the court directs. A common example is an order that the spouse with custody of the children is to have exclusive possession of the home until all the children are grown, following which the home is to be sold and the net proceeds divided between the spouses.

The court also has the power to vary or discharge an order for exclusive possession at a later date. This will only be done if there has been a material change in the circumstances since the date of the original order. For example, if the wife is granted exclusive possession of the home and she later allows a boyfriend or second husband to move in with her, the court may discharge the order or vary it by requiring the wife to purchase her husband's share of the home or sell the home and divide the proceeds.

7. Occupancy rent

When one spouse is granted exclusive possession of the matrimonial home, the other spouse may be entitled to compensation for use of his or her share of the home. This compensation is known as "occupancy rent," and is typically calculated as one-half of the market rent for the property.

The right to receive occupancy rent is frequently set-off against the obligation to pay child support or spousal support to the spouse who remains in the home, but this is not always the case. Courts have a wide discretion as to whether or not they will order occupancy rent in any given case; a detailed discussion of these court decisions is beyond the scope of this book. The important thing to remember is that if you are being asked to move out of the matrimonial home, you should raise the issue of your entitlement to occupancy rent in exchange for your agreement to vacate the home.

c. SALE OR MORTGAGE OF THE MATRIMONIAL HOME

1. Prohibition on sale without consent

The right to equal possession of the matrimonial home would not exist if the spouse who owned the property could simply sell it to a third party, who could evict the non-owning spouse. To prevent this from happening, the Family Law Act prohibits a person from selling or mortgaging the home without the written consent of his or her spouse.

The non-owning spouse must sign a consent on the deed or mortgage before the property can be registered in the name of the purchaser or mortgagee.

2. What if my spouse does not consent?

If your spouse is unreasonably refusing to consent to a sale or mortgage of the home, you may apply to court for an order dispensing with the consent. The court will not intervene if there is simply a disagreement between the spouses about whether the transaction should be completed. There must be clear evidence that the refusal to consent is unreasonable. The consent of a spouse may also be dispensed with if he or she cannot be found or does not have the mental capacity to consent.

3. Can my spouse lie about being married?

Suppose the wife owns the home and wants to sell it to raise money for a business venture. The husband is opposed to the venture and will not consent to the sale. To complete the transaction, the wife tells the purchaser that she is not married and that the man living in the house is merely a boyfriend. Under these circumstances, the sale is valid as long as the purchaser had no knowledge that the wife was married. Of course, the wife is guilty of a criminal offence and liable to her husband for the loss of his right to live in the matrimonial home.

On the other hand, if the purchaser was aware that the wife was married and proceeded to purchase the home without the husband's consent, the court can set aside the sale and declare it null and void.

6

DIVISION OF FAMILY PROPERTY

a. THE PRINCIPLE OF EQUAL DIVISION

The basic idea behind the division of family property is that you and your spouse have made an equal contribution to the marriage. The contribution may consist of child care and housework inside the home, or it may consist of financial support from working outside the home. It may be a little of each. Regardless of where the work was performed, you and your spouse are deemed to have made an equal contribution. As a result, if the marriage dissolves, you are each entitled to an equal share of the net family property. If one spouse owns more net family property than the other, an equalizing payment must be made.

b. HOW IS NET FAMILY PROPERTY CALCULATED?

Net family property consists of the total increase in each spouse's net worth while they were married and living together. It also includes each spouse's interest in the matrimonial home (whenever it was acquired).

To calculate this amount, you need to find out your net worth as of the date of marriage and deduct it from your net worth as of the date of separation. First add up the total value of property owned by you on the day you and your spouse separated. Include any vehicles or land registered in your name, your share of the matrimonial home and its contents, your interest in any business or corporation, your jewellery and other personal items, and any investments, such as stocks, bonds, or savings accounts. Do not include gifts or inheritances received from a third party, money received from the proceeds of a claim for personal injuries, or proceeds of a life insurance policy. From this total, deduct all your outstanding debts to arrive at your net worth as of the date of separation.

Next, deduct your debts on the date of marriage from the value of all property, except the matrimonial home, that you owned on that date. Deduct this total from your net worth as of the date of separation. The resulting amount is your net family property. It represents the increase in your net worth during the marriage.

After you and your spouse have each calculated your own net family property, the spouse with the higher net family property is obliged to pay one-half of the difference to the spouse with the lower net family property. The purpose of this equalization payment is to ensure that the property acquired by the spouses during their marriage has been equally divided.

Sample #6 shows a simple example of how this division of family property works. However, in a real situation some of the following problems may come up.

1.   Who owns what?

When a couple is happily married, they rarely pay attention to the individual ownership of various items purchased during the marriage. Even if they can remember which spouse actually bought the item, the money may have come from the other spouse, or it may have come from a joint account to which both spouses contributed. The best approach may be to assume equal ownership of such items.

A similar problem may come up when you and your spouse list your property and debts on the date of your marriage, which must be deducted from net family property. If the marriage was a long time ago, it may be difficult to recall what your debts and your assets were as of that date.

SAMPLE #6
DIVISION OF FAMILY PROPERTY

John and Mary were married in 1971. They separated in 1994.

DIVISION OF FAMILY PROPERTY

	Husband	Wife
Property owned on date of separation		
Matrimonial home (jointly owned)	75 000	$ 75 000
Furniture (jointly owned)	8 000	8 000
1992 Nissan	15 000	
1989 station wagon		7 000
Canada Savings Bonds	10 000	
Coin collection	2 000	
Sailboat	10 000	
Bell Canada shares	6 000	
Jewellery		10 000
TOTAL property owned at separation	$126 000	$100 000
Family debts at separation		
Husband's car loan	6 000	
Mortgage (joint debt of $60 000)	30 000	30 000
TOTAL debts	36 000	30 000
NET WORTH AT SEPARATION:	90 000	70 000
Property owned on date of marriage		
1966 Volkswagen	500	
Canada Savings Bonds	9 000	
Coin collection	1 000	
Cash	12 000	5 000
Jewellery		5 000
TOTAL property on date of marriage	22 500	10 000
Debts on date of marriage		
Student loan	(2 500)	NIL
NET WORTH ON DATE OF MARRIAGE:	20 000	10 000
Net family property (net worth at separation minus net worth on date of marriage)	70 000	60 000
Equalization payment	(5 000)	5 000
NET FAMILY PROPERTY AFTER EQUALIZATION PAYMENT:	65 000	65 000

Wedding gifts in particular will be a problem, as you will have to distinguish between gifts given before and gifts given after the wedding and between gifts given to you exclusively and gifts given to you and your spouse jointly.

If you are planning to get married or have just recently been married, you and your spouse would be wise to record and agree on this information while it is still fresh in your minds.

2. What is included in my property?

For purposes of property division, your property includes anything of value that you own. This refers not only to physical items, such as a house or a car, but also to savings accounts, investments, corporate shareholdings, business interests, RRSPs, pension rights, and other intangibles. It also includes property that has been placed in someone else's name but that you control.

As stated earlier, there are certain items that do not form part of net family property. These include gifts and inheritances received during the marriage from third parties, damage awards for personal injuries, and proceeds of a life insurance policy. With very few other exceptions, everything else that you own on the date of separation is included in the calculation of net family property for which you must account to your spouse.

When calculating your net family property, remember that the matrimonial home is not excluded even though it may have been owned by one of the spouses before the marriage. The result is that the matrimonial home will always be divided equally unless it is excluded by a special court order or by agreement between the spouses.

3. How do I value my property?

Placing a value on your property can be very difficult. In particular, intangible items such as business interests, minority shareholdings, and pensions present valuation problems that cannot be dealt with by a layperson or, for that matter, by most lawyers. In these cases, you will need an appraiser, actuary, or other person skilled in valuation to assist you in placing a value on your net family property.

c. IS NET FAMILY PROPERTY ALWAYS DIVIDED EQUALLY?

There are times when an equal division of family property is clearly unfair. For example, suppose a husband and wife each began marriage with $15 000 in separate bank accounts. During the marriage, the wife carefully invested her money so that ten years later it had increased to $30 000. The husband, on the other hand, squandered his savings on reckless investments and annual gambling junkets. If the spouses separated after ten years, the normal rules of property division would entitle the husband to half of the increase in the wife's savings, or $7 500. Most people would consider this unfair.

As another example, consider the case of a wealthy middle-aged man who married a woman many years his junior. The couple had lived in the husband's million-dollar mansion for two years when the husband discovered his wife was having an affair. He sued for divorce on the grounds of adultery. The normal rules of property division would entitle the wife to half of the matrimonial home, even though the home was acquired by the husband before the marriage. Once again, this appears to be patently unfair.

In the above situations and any other case where an equal division of net family property would be unconscionable, the court has the power to make an unequal division or no division at all.

d. HOW IS A PENSION DIVIDED?

Many people working in Ontario have two pension plans. One is the Canada Pension Plan, which all employees must contribute to and be members of. The other is a private pension plan offered as a benefit of employment.

In each case, the pension consists of a monthly payment to the employee commencing after he or she retires. Before retirement, the employee usually does not receive any payment or other benefit from the pension. When a pension holder separates from his or her spouse, the division of the pension often receives special treatment. This is because the pension is not a tangible asset that can be sold at the time of separation.

In the case of the Canada Pension Plan, either party to the separation may apply under the Canada Pension Plan Act for a division of pension credits. For spouses who separated after 1987, the application may be brought 12 months after the date of separation. The effect of the application is to total the pension credits earned by both spouses while they were living together, and allocate half of those credits to each spouse. As a result, the spouse who made greater contributions to the pension plan would receive a reduced pension on retirement, and the spouse who made lesser contributions would receive an increased pension. However, the spouses would not necessarily receive an equal pension on retirement because the contributions made before they lived together and after separation are not divided. A division of Canada Pension Plan credits is also available to common-law spouses who lived together for at least one year before they separated.

In the case of a private pension plan, there is no method available for dividing pension credits at the source. As a result, two procedures have developed for dividing a private pension.

Under the first method, an actuary is hired to calculate the value of the pension as of the date of the separation. This complex calculation determines the value at a fixed point in time of a stream of periodic payments that will commence at a later date. The calculation depends largely on assumptions as to interest rates, indexing of pension payments, inflation rates, and tax rates. The valuation of the pension can change substantially, depending on what assumptions are made on these and similar matters. Determining the exact present value of the pension is therefore a matter of negotiation between the spouses. If the spouses cannot agree, the only alternative is to apply to the court.

Once the present value of the pension is fixed, the amount is added to the net family property of the pensionholder. In order to equalize net family property, one-half of the present value of the pension would have to be paid to the other spouse (unless the other spouse has assets that would offset the value of the pension).

The difficulty with the first method is that the pensionholder must pay his or her spouse one-half of the value of the pension in a lump sum, even though the pension may not be received for several years. As a result, a second procedure has developed which is known as an "if and when" settlement. Under this system, no monies are paid by the pensionholder until he or she begins to receive the pension. When the pension payments begin, the pensionholder pays his or her spouse a monthly periodic payment to satisfy the claim. The details of an "if and when" settlement agreement are very complex, and you should not attempt such an agreement without the help of a lawyer who is experienced in this area.

e. WHAT IF WE DON'T WANT OUR PROPERTY EQUALLY DIVIDED?

The Family Law Act does not impose the division of property rules on couples who do not want them. If the husband and wife are in agreement about what they want done with their property, they can sign a marriage contract setting their own terms.

Even if a couple does not have a marriage contract, they may divide the family property in any way that is mutually agreeable and put the terms of the division into a separation agreement. The key word in both cases is "agree." If the couple cannot agree on how their property should be divided, the property will be divided as described above according to the Family Law Act.

It should be noted that the division of a pension under the Canada Pension Plan cannot be altered by means of a marriage contract or separation agreement. The Canada Pension Plan is a federal statute that prevails over the Family Law Act, and does not allow the spouses to release their rights to a division of the federal pension. This is not the case with respect to private employers' pensions, which are often released in separation agreements.

f. HOW DO I ENFORCE MY PROPERTY RIGHTS?

If you and your spouse are separated, and there is no reasonable prospect of a reconciliation, either one of you may apply to court for a division of your property in accordance with the Family Law Act. The court has the power to order the spouse with the higher net family property to make an equalizing payment to the other spouse where necessary. The court can secure payment by placing a mortgage on any property owned by the spouse.

The application to court can be made any time within six years following the separation. However, if you are divorced, the application must be brought no later than two years after the divorce becomes final.

g. WHAT IF MY SPOUSE DIES?

When a spouse dies, the marriage has come to an end. The law gives the surviving spouse the same property rights that he or she would have had if the marriage had ended through separation or divorce.

If the net family property of the deceased spouse (calculated as of the day before he or she died) exceeds the net family property of the surviving spouse, the surviving spouse may claim an equalizing payment from the estate.

In practice, property claims arising from the death of a spouse are rare because the spouse who died usually leaves all of his or her property to the surviving spouse by will. In such cases, the surviving spouse already owns everything and would have nothing to gain by making a property claim under the Family Law Act.

If your spouse dies without a will or if the will does not leave everything to you, you must make a choice. You can elect to take what has been left to you by the will or by the law of intestate succession, which divides among the relatives the property of a person who dies without a will, or you can claim an equalizing payment from the estate, just as if you and your spouse had separated.

In deciding which route to take, you should consider the amount of money you would receive under the will (or intestate succession laws) as opposed to the amount you would receive under the Family Law Act. This may involve several complicated calculations; you will probably need the help of a lawyer or accountant to arrive at the figure.

You should also keep in mind that a claim under a will is far less controversial because you are receiving property your deceased spouse voluntarily left you. A claim under the Family Law Act could very well result in complicated and possibly hostile litigation with the other beneficiaries of the estate.

h. THE FINANCIAL STATEMENT

An application to court for division of family property will not be successful unless there is a detailed disclosure of each spouse's assets and liabilities as of the date of marriage and as of the date of separation or death. The Family Law Act requires each spouse to complete a standard form known as a financial statement which sets out all this information (see Sample #7). When the financial statement is completed, the spouses must verify under oath that the information is all true to the best of their knowledge.

When you complete a financial statement, you must make sure that it is accurate and that you have not suppressed

71

any relevant information. Your failure to provide accurate information could result in serious consequences for you.

If you are asking for support or division of assets, both spouses will have to file a financial statement. To get your spouse to fill out the appropriate form, send a notice to file financial statement (see the final page of Sample #7). Your spouse must file this form within the same time limits for filing an answer to the petition (noted on the first page of the petition).

SAMPLE #7
FINANCIAL STATEMENT
ONTARIO COURT (GENERAL DIVISION)

Court file no. _____

ONTARIO COURT (GENERAL DIVISION)

BETWEEN:

JOAN PUBLIC   PETITIONER, (Wife   )

- and -

JOHN QUE PUBLIC   RESPONDENT (Husband   )

FINANCIAL STATEMENT

I, ____Joan Public____ of the ____City____
  (full name of deponent)   (city, town, etc.)

of ____Toronto____ in the ____Municipality____
  (county, municipality, etc.)

of ____Metropolitan Toronto____ make oath and say:
  /affirm:

1. Particulars of my financial situation and of all my property are accurately set out below, to the best of my knowledge, information, and belief.

ALL INCOME AND MONEY RECEIVED

(Include all income and other money received from all sources, whether taxable or not. Show gross amount here and show deductions on pages 2, 3, 4 & 5. Give current actual amount where known or ascertainable. Where amount cannot be ascertained, give your best estimate. Use weekly, monthly or yearly column as appropriate.)

Category	Weekly	Monthly	Yearly
1. Salary or wages		$2 000.00	
2. Bonuses			
3. Fees			
4. Commissions			
5. Family allowance		27.00	
6. Unemployment insurance			
7. Workers' compensation			
8. Public assistance			
9. Pension			
10. Dividends			
11. Interest			
12. Rental income			
13. Allowances and support from others			
14. Other (Specify)			
TOTAL	$	(A)$ 2 027.00	$

Weekly total $_____ × 4.33 = (B)$_____ monthly

Yearly total $_____ ÷ 12 = (C)$_____ monthly

GROSS MONTHLY INCOME (A) + (B) + (C) = (D)$ 2 027.00 _____

OTHER BENEFITS

(Show all non-monetary benefits from all sources, such as use of a vehicle or room and board, and include such items as insurance or dental plans or other expenses paid on your behalf. Give your best estimate where you cannot ascertain the actual value.)

Item	Particulars	Monthly market value

TOTAL (E) $ _____

GROSS MONTHLY INCOME AND BENEFITS (D) + (E) = $ 2 027.00

ACTUAL AND PROPOSED BUDGETS

ACTUAL BUDGET

for twelve month period from
_____ June 1 _____ , 19 _____
to _____ June 1 _____ , 19 _____
Show actual expenses, or your best estimate where you cannot ascertain actual amount.

PROPOSED BUDGET

Show your proposed budget, giving your best estimate where you cannot ascertain actual amount.

CATEGORY	Weekly	Monthly	Yearly	Weekly	Monthly	Yearly
Housing						
Rent		$1 000.00				
Real property taxes						1 200.00
Mortgage					1 000.00	
Common expense charges						
Water		15.00			15.00	
Electricity		20.00			20.00	
Natural gas		100.00			100.00	
Fuel oil						
Telephone		25.00			25.00	
Cable TV		20.00			20.00	
Home insurance			600.00			600.00
Repairs and maintenance			100.00			100.00
Gardening and snow removal						
Other (specify)						
Food, toiletries and sundries						
Groceries	50.00			75.00		
Meals outside home	10.00			20.00		
Toiletries and sundries	20.00			25.00		
Grooming	20.00			30.00		

CATEGORY	ACTUAL BUDGET			PROPOSED BUDGET		
Food Tolletries and Sundries — cont'd	Weekly	Monthly	Yearly	Weekly	Monthly	Yearly
General household supplies	20.00			25.00		
Laundry, dry cleaning	10.00			20.00		
Other (specify)						
Clothing						
Children		100.00			200.00	
Self		100.00			200.00	
Transportation						
Public transit		150.00			150.00	
Taxis, car pools	10.00			20.00		
Car insurance			450.00			450.00
Licence			70.00			70.00
Car maintenance			500.00			500.00
Gasoline, oil	20.00					
Parking	5.00					
Other (specify)						
Health and Medical						
Doctors, chiropractors						
Dentist (regular care)		120.00				200.00
Orthodontist or special dental care						1 000.00
Insurance premiums			720.00			720.00
Drugs						
Other (specify)						
Deductions from Income						
Income tax		500.00			500.00	
Canada Pension Plan		30.00			30.00	
Unemployment insurance		30.00			30.00	
Employer pension						
Union or other dues						

CATEGORY	ACTUAL BUDGET			PROPOSED BUDGET		
Deductions from income — con't.	Weekly	Monthly	Yearly	Weekly	Monthly	Yearly
Group insurance						
Credit union loan						
Credit union savings						
Other (specify)						
Miscellaneous						
Life insurance premiums			200.00			200.00
Tuition fees, books, etc.						
Entertainment	10.00			20.00		
Recreation	10.00			20.00		
Vacation			0			500.00
Gifts			0			500.00
Babysitting, day care	50.00			75.00		
Children's allowances						
Children's activities	10.00			20.00		
Support payments						
Newspapers, periodicals		10.00			10.00	
Alcohol, tobacco		50.00			75.00	
Charities						
Income tax (not deducted at source)						
Other (specify)						
Loan payments						
Banks						
Finance companies						
Credit unions						
Department stores						
Other (specify)						

CATEGORY	ACTUAL BUDGET			PROPOSED BUDGET		
Savings	Weekly	Monthly	Yearly	Weekly	Monthly	Yearly
RRSP						
Other (specify)						
	$	$	$	$	$	$

TOTALS OF ACTUAL BUDGET

Monthly Total $ 2 150.00

Weekly Total $ _____ x 4.33 = $ 1 060.85

Yearly Total $ _____ ÷ 12 = $ 230.00

MONTHLY ACTUAL BUDGET   = (F) $ 3 440.85

TOTALS OF PROPOSED BUDGET

Monthly Total $ 2 375.00

Weekly Total $ 380.___ x 4.33 = $ 1 645.00

Yearly Total $ 6 040.00 ÷ 12 = $ 503.55

MONTHLY PROPOSED BUDGET   = (G) $ 4 523.95

SUMMARY OF INCOME AND EXPENSES

Actual

Gross monthly income
(Amount D from page 1) $ 2 027.00

Subtract monthly actual budget
(Amount F from page 5) $ 3 400.85

ACTUAL MONTHLY SURPLUS/DEFICIT $ 1 413.75

Proposed

Gross monthly income
(Amount D from page 1) $ 2 027.00

Subtract proposed monthly budget
(Amount G from page 5) $ 4 523.95

PROPOSED MONTHLY SURPLUS/DEFICIT $ 2 496.95

LAND

(Include any interest in land owned on the valuation date including leasehold interests and mortgages whether or not you are registered as owner. Include claims to an interest in land, but do not include claims that you are making against your spouse in this or a related proceeding. Show estimated market value of your interest without deducting encumbrances or costs of disposition, and show encumbrances and costs of disposition under Debts and Other Liabilities.)

Nature and type ownership *(State percentage interest where relevant)*	Nature and address of property	Estimated market value of your interest as of: *(See instructions above)*		
		Date of marriage	Valuation date	Date of statement
Joint Tenancy 50%	Matrimonial Home, 322 Lakeside Rd., Toronto, ON	62 500.00	67 500.	70 000.
	TOTAL $	62 500.00	(H) 67 500.	70 000.

GENERAL HOUSEHOLD ITEMS AND VEHICLES

(Show estimated market value, not cost of replacement, for these items owned on the valuation date. Do not deduct encumbrances here, but show encumbrances under Debts and Other Liabilities.)

Item	Particulars	Estimated market value of your interest as of: *(See instructions above)*		
		Date of marriage	Valuation date	Date of statement
General household contents excluding special items				
(a) at matrimonial home(s)	Refrigerator, stove, washer dryer, furniture, etc.	10 000	8 000.	5 000.
(b) elsewhere				
Jewellery	diamond ring (gift)	1 000.	1 200.	1 400.
Works of art				
Vehicles and boats	1984 Station wagon	15 000.	13 000.	10 000.
Other special items				
	TOTAL $	26 000.00	22 200.00	16 400.00

SAVINGS AND SAVINGS PLANS

(Show items owned on the valuation date by category. Include cash, accounts in financial institutions, registered retirement or other savings plans, deposit receipts, pensions, and any other savings.)

Category	Institution	Account number	Date of marriage	Amount as of: Valuation date	Date of statement
None					

TOTAL $ _____ (J) _____

SECURITIES

(Show items owned on the valuation date by category. Include shares, bonds, warrants, options, debentures, notes, and any other securities. Give your best estimate of market value if the items were to be sold on an open market.)

Category	Number	Description	Date of marriage	Estimated market value as of: Valuation date	Date of statement
None					

TOTAL $ _____ (K) _____

LIFE AND DISABILITY INSURANCE

(List all policies owned on the valuation date.)

Company and policy no.	Kind of policy	Owner	Beneficiary	Face amount	Date of marriage	Cash surrender value as of: Valuation date	Date of statement
INS Co.	Life	Self	Child	100 000.	no cash	surrender	value

TOTAL $ _____ (L) _____

ACCOUNTS RECEIVABLE

(Give particulars of all debts owing to you on the valuation date, whether arising from business or from personal dealings.)

		Amount as of:		
Particulars		Date of marriage	Valuation date	Date of statement
None				
	TOTAL $		(M)	

BUSINESS INTERESTS

(Show any interest in an unincorporated business owned on the valuation date. A controlling interest in an incorporated business may be shown here or under Securities. Give your best estimate of market value if the business were to be sold on an open market.)

		Estimated market value as of:		
Name of firm or company	Interest	Date of marriage	Valuation date	Date of statement
None				
	TOTAL $		(N)	

OTHER PROPERTY

(Show other property owned on the valuation date by categories. Include property of any kind not shown here. Give your best estimate of market value.)

		Estimated market value as of:		
Category	Particulars	Date of marriage	Valuation date	Date of statement
None				
	TOTAL $		(O)	

DEBTS AND OTHER LIABILITIES

(Show your debts and other liabilities on the valuation date, whether arising from personal or business dealings, by category such as mortgages, charges, liens, notes, credit cards, and accounts payable. Include contingent liabilities such as guarantees and indicate that they are contingent.)

			Amount as of:	
Category	Particulars	Date of marriage	Valuation date	Date of statement
None				

TOTAL $

PROPERTY, DEBTS, AND OTHER LIABILITIES ON DATE OF MARRIAGE

(Show by category the value of your property and your debts and other liabilities calculated as of the date of your marriage. Do not include the value of a matrimonial home that you owned at the date of marriage.)

		Value as of date of marriage	
Category	Particulars	Assets	Liabilities
None			

TOTAL $ (Q) $ _____   (R) $ _____

NET VALUE OF PROPERTY OWNED ON DATE OF MARRIAGE (Amount Q Subtract Amount R) = (S) $ _____

SAMPLE #7 — Continued

EXCLUDED PROPERTY

(Show the value by category of property owned on the valuation date that is excluded from the definition of "net family property.")

Category	Particulars	Value on Valuation Date
Gift	Diamond ring	1 200.00

TOTAL   (T) $ 1 200.00

DISPOSAL OF PROPERTY

(Show the value by category of all property that you disposed of during the two years immediately preceding the making of this statement, or during the marriage, whichever period is shorter.)

Category	Particulars	Value
None		

TOTAL   (U) $

CALCULATION OF NET FAMILY PROPERTY

Value of all property owned on valuation date (Amounts H, I, J, K, L, M, N, and O) $ 89 700.00

Subtract value of all deductions (Amounts P and S) $ _____

Subtract value of all excluded property (Amount T) $ 1 200.00

NET FAMILY PROPERTY $ 88 500.00

2.   The name(s) and address(es) of my employer(s) are:

      Self-employed

3.   Attached to this affidavit are a copy of my income tax return filed with the Department of National Revenue for the last taxation year, together with all material filed with it, and a copy of any notice of assessment or reassessment that I have received from the Department for that year.

4.   I do not anticipate any material changes in the information set out above.

OR

4.   I anticipate the following material changes in the information set out above:

SWORN/AFFIRMED BEFORE ME at the

City of _____ Toronto _____

in the Municipality of _Metropolitan Toronto_

this _____ day of _____ 19 ____.   _____ *Joan Que Publi*
                                                    Signature

I. M. Commissioner

A Commissioner for taking Affidavits, etc.

Court file no._____

ONTARIO COURT (GENERAL DIVISION)

BETWEEN:

PETITIONER

Joan   Public   (Wife   )

- and -

(Court seal)

John Que Public   RESPONDENT

(Husband   )

NOTICE TO FILE FINANCIAL STATEMENT

TO: John Que Public

In this proceeding a claim has been made against you for__support_____

YOU ARE REQUIRED, WHETHER OR NOT YOU DEFEND THIS PROCEEDING, to serve and file a financial statement in Form 70N prescribed by the Rules of Civil Procedure. Your financial statement must accompany your responding document if you defend this proceeding and must be served and filed in any event within the time for delivering your responding document after the original process in this proceeding was served on you.

If you fail to file a financial statement as required, an order may be made without further notice to compel you to file a financial statement.

Joan   Public

_____   322 Lakeshore Road

Date   Toronto, Ontario

555-5556

Petitioner appearing in person

To:

John Que Public

1000 Yonge Street

Toronto, Ontario

INTERNATIONAL SELF-COUNSEL PRESS LTD.
1481 Charlotte Road
North Vancouver, B.C. V7J 1H1
DIVONT-SOLE (3-1) 91

7

SUPPORT

a. SUPPORT IN GENERAL

1. The duty to pay support

The duty to pay support came into being because of the state of dependency within the family unit. This simply means that some members of a family have come to rely or depend upon other members of a family for financial provision. The most obvious example is a child who relies entirely on his or her parents for financial needs. Similarly, a parent who remains at home to look after young children is often dependent upon his or her spouse to provide money for the family. Finally, there is the less common situation where an elderly parent is financially dependent upon his or her adult children.

In all of these cases, the law protects the dependent party by ensuring that financial support will continue even though the family unit may have broken up.

2. When do support obligations begin?

In the case of a child, the obligation to provide support begins when the child is born. In the case of a spouse, it can begin as early as the date of the marriage. If the parties are not married, the obligation to provide spousal support arises after three years of continuous cohabitation or after a child is born of the relationship. In practical terms, support payments are usually not claimed until the spouses are separated. If there are children, the spouse with custody of the children is entitled to claim child support as well as spousal support.

As long as the parties are married, the obligation to provide support and the amount of the support payments is covered by the Family Law Act. But if one of the spouses files for divorce, the obligation to pay support is governed by the Divorce Act.

Support for an ex-spouse should relieve economic hardship arising from the breakdown of the marriage, recognize any economic advantages or disadvantages arising from the roles played by the spouses during the marriage, and promote the economic self-sufficiency of each spouse within a reasonable period of time.

It often happens that by the time one of the spouses petitions for a divorce, the questions of support, custody, or access have already been dealt with either by court order or by a separation agreement. If both spouses are content with the previous order or agreement, and the matter is not raised in the divorce proceeding, the previous order or agreement continues in effect. But if a request regarding support, custody, or access is made in the divorce proceeding, the court is not bound by the prior order or agreement and can change it as it thinks fit.

The divorce court can disregard the previous support arrangements and may order more or fewer support payments than were previously being paid. The court can order support for an ex-spouse, for a child of the marriage, or for both, and can order security to ensure that the support is paid. The court is not likely to change the previous agreement if there have been no real changes in circumstances.

If the divorce court does not deal with the question of support, a support order made under the Family Law Act will remain in effect even though the parties are no longer married.

3. How are support payments made?

The most common type of support is a regular monthly or weekly amount paid by one spouse to the other. However, support payments can be made once a year or as a one-time lump sum payment. The court can also require one spouse to pay specific expenses of the other spouse, such as rent, mortgage, or utilities.

If the support is being paid under a court order, it must be paid to the office of the director of the family support plan who will forward the money directly to the dependent spouse. Support paid under a separation agreement can also be paid through the director's office if a copy of the agreement is filed in the family court. The advantage of this arrangement is that the director will keep an accurate record of what payments have been made and what arrears are outstanding and will enforce collection of the arrears, if necessary.

4. The amount of support

How much support is enough? The answer to this question seems to differ greatly depending on whether you are the receiving spouse or the paying spouse! The spouse claiming support sometimes demands an outrageous amount, while the spouse on the paying end only agrees to pay a small amount or nothing at all. If both spouses remain stubborn in their positions, they will end up in a costly and hostile legal battle, which may have a result that neither is happy with. The sensible thing is for each spouse to compromise so they can reach an out-of-court agreement.

The basic criteria the law uses to determine the amount of support are need and the ability to pay. In other words, you calculate the amount of money the dependent spouse needs to maintain his or her standard of living, and require the other spouse to pay as much of that amount as possible without seriously sacrificing his or her standard of living. In the usual case, both parties must reduce their standard of living for the simple reason that it is more expensive to live apart than to live together.

b. SPOUSAL SUPPORT

1. Extended definition of spouse

You do not have to be married to claim spousal support. Two people who are not married but have lived together continuously for at least three years have an obligation to support one another. If the relationship has lasted less than three years but the couple has a child, the support obligation also exists.

2. The obligation of self-support

The major difference between child support and spousal support is that a spouse has an obligation to provide support for himself or herself. A spouse is only entitled to spousal support (as distinct from child support) if that spouse is unable to provide for his or her own support. One of the purposes of a support order is to help the spouse become self-sufficient as soon as possible.

This means that any spouse who is capable of working and earning income is expected to do so following a separation. Support is ordered only if the spouse cannot earn enough income to be self-supporting or for one reason or another is unable to work.

3. Amount of spousal support

The amount of spousal support payable is calculated by looking at the financial need of the dependent spouse and the ability to pay of the other spouse.

In determining the need of the dependent spouse, the court looks at the accustomed standard of living of the parties. For example, consider a woman married to a millionaire and accustomed to a high standard of living before her separation. Although she can support herself as a secretary earning $20 000 a year, she may nevertheless be entitled to spousal support in order to maintain her previous standard of living. If the same woman had been married to a man earning $25 000 a year, she would probably be considered self-sufficient and would not be entitled to spousal support.

In addition to the basic concepts of need and ability to pay, the amount of a spousal support order is also affected by the following factors:

(a) The length of time the spouses cohabited: If the marriage is short, the state of dependency described earlier may not have had time to develop. As a result, the obligation to pay support is decreased.

(b) The effect of child care and other responsibilities on one spouse's earning capacity: If one of the spouses worked while the other remained at home to look after the house and the children, the spouse who remained at home will almost certainly have a lower earning capacity due to the lack of employable job skills. This is precisely the type of dependency that a support order is intended to overcome, and the amount of support should be high enough to overcome the diminished earning capacity of the dependent spouse.

Recent court decisions have placed great emphasis on the need to compensate a spouse, usually the wife, for financial disadvantages resulting from the role she played in the marriage, in raising children, and in looking after the home. The courts acknowledge that following divorce, many women are financially worse off than their husbands, and describe this phenomenon as the "feminization of poverty." The courts have held that if the marriage conferred an economic disadvantage on the wife, the wife should be compensated by way of support payments, so that the economic advantages and disadvantages of the marriage are borne equally by both spouses.

(c) The value of housekeeping and child care: Under the Family Law Act, a spouse may assert that his or her housekeeping or child care services are equal in value to the employed spouse's income. The spouse may claim the right to continue to work in the home and seek an amount of support money enabling him or her to do so. Of course, this is only possible where the spouse paying support earns enough income to financially support two households. In many cases, it is not practical for either spouse to remain at home after a separation because the increased cost of living apart requires both spouses to obtain a paying job.

4. The causal connection — court interpretation of the law of support

Although the law of spousal support is set out in the Family Law Act and the Divorce Act, the power to interpret and apply these laws is left to the courts.

In recent years, some of the cases emerging from the courts have suggested a change in the law that has come to be known as "the causal connection." In general terms, this means that a spouse may only be entitled to support if the cause of his or her dependency is connected to or generated by the marriage.

For example, consider a case where the spouses both worked during the marriage and were earning about the same income when they separated. Six months later one of them is laid off and needs support. A plain reading of the Family Law Act would entitle that spouse to apply for support from his or her marriage partner. But some courts have refused to order support in these circumstances because there is no causal connection between the marriage and the spouse's need for support. The logic behind this is that once the spouses are separated and self-sufficient, the obligation to assist the needy spouse falls on the government and the community, not on the other spouse.

Many of the so-called causal connection cases arise as a result of an application to vary an existing support order or separation agreement. The Divorce Act and the Family Law Act both allow for variation due to a material change in the circumstances of one of the spouses. But once again, there have been court cases that refuse the variation if the change in circumstances is unrelated to the marriage.

For example, a dependent spouse may have been working for the minimum wage prior to separation and agreed to a monthly support payment from her spouse to supplement her income. She later becomes disabled, is forced to give up the job, and therefore applies to the court to increase the support payments due to the change in circumstances. Under the principle of law which requires a causal connection between the disability and the marriage, the application would probably be unsuccessful.

A recent decision of the Supreme Court of Canada suggests that the causal connection rule is limited to situations where the parties had negotiated a final separation agreement. If one of them later seeks to increase or decrease the support because of a change in circumstances, he or she would not be permitted to do so unless the change was connected in some way to the marriage.

Because the court cases dealing with spousal support differ greatly in their application of the causal connection rule, it is difficult to predict how this principle will be applied to an individual case. However, spouses who receive or pay support should be aware of the causal connection rule and how their rights may be affected by it.

c. CHILD SUPPORT

1. Who pays child support?

Although both parents have a duty to support their children, it is generally the parent who does not have custody who pays the child support to the parent with custody. The parent with custody receives the money on behalf of the child and uses it for the child's financial needs. In theory, however, a child could apply to court for an order that both parents be required to support him or her financially.

For purposes of child support claims, a child includes not only a natural child but also anyone treated by a parent as a child of the family, for example, a spouse's child from a previous marriage.

2. Duration of child support

Generally speaking, the duty to provide child support ends when the child reaches 18 years of age. However, there are at least three exceptions to this rule:

(a) A child over 18 who is enrolled in a full-time program of education is entitled to child support if he or she has not withdrawn from parental control.

(b) A child over 16 who has withdrawn from parental control is not entitled to child support.

(c) A child of any age who is married is not entitled to child support.

3. Amount of child support

An order for support of a child normally recognizes that both parents have an obligation to support the child according to the financial capability of each parent.

The calculation of child support payments is a two-step process. First, calculate the total cost of supporting the child, including money spent directly on the child as well as the child's portion of general household expenses. Depending on your standard of living, this amount could be anywhere from $200 to $1 000 per month, or possibly more. You then divide the support payment between you and your spouse proportionate to your respective incomes.

Consider the following example:

Father's income per month: $1 750

Mother's income per month: $1 150

Total monthly income of both parents: $2 900

Wife's proportion of total income:

$$\frac{\$1\ 150}{\$2\ 900} \times 100\% = 40\% \text{ (approx.)}$$

Husband's proportion of total income:

$$\frac{\$1\ 750}{\$2\ 900} \times 100\% = 60\% \text{ (approx.)}$$

Cost per month of supporting child: $ 500

Husband's support obligation (if wife has custody):

$500   x   60% = $300

Wife's support obligation (if husband has custody):

$500   x   40% = $200

Although the above calculation is a useful guideline to determine child support obligations, it is by no means fixed. There are a number of factors the court considers in deciding the amount of child support. Some of these are as follows:

(a) Each parent's capacity to provide support: In the above example, the child's mother earns a monthly income of only $1 150. The mother's basic costs of supporting herself would use up all or most of that amount, leaving very little money for child support. If the father had custody, the mother would probably not be liable to pay much child support unless her income increased.

(b) Each parent's expenses: Although everyone has basic expenses, such as housing, food, and clothing, one parent may have additional special expenses, such as loan payments, medical bills, transportation costs, and prior support obligations. It is essential to consider both the income and the expenses of the parents before fixing the amount of child support.

(c) Second families: If the parent paying support marries or lives with someone else and has more children, the parent must then support both the first family and the second family. Generally speaking, the rights of the first family have priority, but there are no hard and fast rules for dividing the support obligation in this type of case.

(d) Second spouses: If the parent receiving support remarries and lives with someone earning another income, that parent's expenses may well go down due to the contribution of his or her new spouse. Moreover, the new spouse will often become a parent figure to the child and acquire child support obligations. In these circumstances, the natural parent paying child support may be required to pay less.

4. Federal guidelines

The government of Canada has released guidelines for monthly child support payments which are geared to the income of the parent paying support. The guidelines are intended to reduce conflict between parents and to establish fairer and more consistent child support payments throughout the country. They are expected to take effect on May 1, 1997, and are shown in Table #2.

5. Are child support payments tax deductible?

Child support payments under an order or agreement which was made before May 1, 1997, are tax deductible to the payor and taxable to the recipient. That is, the person paying the support can deduct the amount paid from income for tax purposes, while the person receiving it must include the amount received as taxable income. Child support payments under orders or agreements made after May 1, 1997, are not tax deductible to the payor and are not taxable to the recipient.

The child support payment guidelines shown in Table #2 take effect on May 1, 1997, and are calculated on the basis that no tax will be deducted from or paid on the amounts shown in the table. If you are a party to a support order made before May 1, 1997, you may apply to the court to have your order varied to reflect the guidelines and the new tax rules.

d. OBTAINING A SUPPORT ORDER

1. Filing a domestic contract

If you and your spouse are able to agree on the amount of support to be paid (spousal or child), you should set out your agreement in a written domestic contract. (See chapter 3 for a description and sample domestic contract.) You will probably need a lawyer to help you prepare this document.

The domestic contract should then be filed in the nearest branch of the Ontario Court (Provincial Division), commonly known as the Family Court. The support obligation in the domestic contract will have the same force and effect as a court order to pay support.

2. Application for support

If you and your spouse cannot agree on the amount of support or if your spouse simply refuses to pay support, you will have to apply to court for a support order. The application may be brought in the Ontario Court (Provincial Division) or in the Ontario Court (General Division).

If your claim is only for support or custody and your financial situation is not overly complicated, you are far better off to apply at the provincial level. The provincial courts usually have staff available to help you prepare your claim, and the application forms are easy to complete. Your case will also be heard fairly quickly. In the general division it can take much longer and you will almost certainly need a lawyer's assistance. Sample #8 shows an application for support in Provincial Court.

The application for support must be accompanied by a financial statement, which is a detailed description of your income and your expenses (see Sample #9).

When the case reaches trial, the judge will consider the documents filed by both you and your spouse (if your spouse has filed a response to your application) and hear any oral evidence that you both want to give. The judge will then make an order fixing the amount of support to be paid. If no support is to be paid, the application will be dismissed.

After the support order is pronounced, a written support order must be prepared by you or your lawyer (see Sample #10) and signed and sealed by the clerk of the court. The court staff will generally be pleased to help you if you are preparing the form yourself.

3. Limitation period

The right to claim spousal support does not last forever. You must bring the application for support within two years from the date you and your spouse separate. After two years, you will not be entitled to claim spousal support under the Family Law Act. However, you may still claim support after divorce under the Divorce Act (see section **a.**)

4. What if I am served with an application for support?

If you have been served with an application for support, you should file your own financial statement and dispute any information contained in the application that you disagree with. You should also consult with a lawyer and possibly retain him or her to represent you in court.

e. CHANGING A SUPPORT ORDER

1. Can support orders be varied?

Suppose you are ordered to pay child support of $400 per month. At the time the order is made, you are earning about $2 500 per month and can afford the support payments without much difficulty.

TABLE #2
MONTHLY CHILD SUPPORT PAYMENTS
FROM MAY 1997

1996 Annual Gross Income	Monthy amounts (in dollars) based on number of children					
	One	Two	Three	Four	Five	Six or More
0 - 6 754	0	0	0	0	0	0
6 755 - 7 000	8	9	10	11	11	11
7 001 - 8 000	40	45	50	55	55	55
8 001 - 9 000	71	80	89	99	99	99
9 001 - 10 000	79	93	106	120	120	120
10 001 - 12 000	109	148	170	192	192	192
12 001 - 14 000	119	202	232	262	262	262
14 001 - 16 000	131	238	293	332	332	332
16 001 - 18 000	143	261	355	402	402	402
18 001 - 20 000	166	285	388	472	472	472
20 001 - 22 000	197	308	420	512	542	542
22 001 - 24 000	217	338	452	551	612	612
24 001 - 26 000	235	378	484	590	678	682
26 001 - 28 000	249	413	515	623	718	743
28 001 - 30 000	262	439	554	655	755	800
30 001 - 32 000	273	457	585	686	782	839
32 001 - 34 000	288	481	625	734	818	887
34 001 - 36 000	304	506	666	784	867	937
36 001 - 38 000	319	531	699	835	919	988
38 001 - 40 000	335	555	730	873	970	1 040
40 001 - 42 000	350	579	762	911	1 022	1 092
42 001 - 44 000	366	603	793	948	1 074	1 143
44 001 - 46 000	382	628	825	987	1 120	1 233
46 001 - 48 000	398	653	858	1 025	1 164	1 280
48 001 - 50 000	414	679	890	1 063	1 207	1 328
50 001 - 52 000	430	704	922	1 101	1 250	1 376
52 001 - 54 000	444	726	952	1 137	1 290	1 420
54 001 - 56 000	458	748	981	1 171	1 330	1 464
56 001 - 58 000	473	772	1 012	1 208	1 371	1 509
58 001 - 60 000	488	795	1 041	1 242	1 410	1 552
60 001 - 62 000	501	817	1 069	1 275	1 447	1 592
62 001 - 64 000	515	838	1 096	1 308	1 483	1 633
64 001 - 66 000	528	858	1 122	1 338	1 519	1 671
66 001 - 68 000	540	878	1 149	1 370	1 554	1 710
68 001 - 70 000	553	898	1 174	1 400	1 588	1 748
70 001 - 72 000	565	918	1 199	1 430	1 623	1 785
72 001 - 74 000	578	938	1 225	1 461	1 657	1 823
74 001 - 76 000	591	958	1 251	1 492	1 692	1 861
76 001 - 78 000	604	978	1 278	1 523	1 727	1 899
78 001 - 80 000	617	998	1 303	1 553	1 761	1 937
80 001 - 82 000	630	1 018	1 330	1 584	1 796	1 975
82 001 - 84 000	643	1 039	1 355	1 615	1 830	2 013

TABLE #2 — Continued

1996 Annual Gross Income	Monthy amounts (in dollars) based on number of children					
	One	Two	Three	Four	Five	Six or More
84 001 - 86 000	656	1 059	1 381	1 645	1 865	2 051
86 001 - 88 000	669	1 079	1 408	1 676	1 900	2 089
88 001 - 90 000	682	1 099	1 433	1 707	1 935	2 127
90 001 - 92 000	695	1 120	1 460	1 738	1 969	2 165
92 001 - 94 000	708	1 140	1 485	1 768	2 004	2 203
94 001 - 96 000	721	1 160	1 512	1 799	2 039	2 241
96 001 - 98 000	734	1 180	1 538	1 830	2 073	2 279
98 001 - 100 000	747	1 200	1 563	1 860	2 108	2 318
100 001 - 102 000	760	1 221	1 590	1 891	2 143	2 355
102 001 - 104 000	773	1 241	1 615	1 922	2 177	2 393
104 001 - 106 000	786	1 261	1 642	1 953	2 212	2 431
106 001 - 108 000	799	1 281	1 668	1 983	2 247	2 470
108 001 - 110 000	812	1 302	1 693	2 014	2 281	2 508
110 001 - 112 000	825	1 322	1 720	2 045	2 316	2 545
112 001 - 114 000	838	1 342	1 745	2 075	2 351	2 583
114 001 - 116 000	851	1 363	1 772	2 106	2 385	2 621
116 001 - 118 000	864	1 383	1 798	2 137	2 420	2 660
118 001 - 120 000	877	1 403	1 824	2 168	2 455	2 698
120 001 - 122 000	890	1 423	1 850	2 199	2 490	2 735
122 001 - 124 000	903	1 443	1 875	2 229	2 524	2 773
124 001 - 126 000	916	1 463	1 902	2 260	2 559	2 812
126 001 - 128 000	929	1 484	1 928	2 291	2 593	2 850
128 001 - 130 000	942	1 504	1 954	2 322	2 628	2 888
130 001 - 132 000	955	1 524	1 980	2 352	2 663	2 925
132 001 - 134 000	968	1 545	2 005	2 383	2 698	2 963
134 001 - 136 000	981	1 565	2 032	2 414	2 732	3 002
136 001 - 138 000	994	1 585	2 058	2 445	2 767	3 040
138 001 - 140 000	1 007	1 605	2 084	2 475	2 802	3 078
140 001 - 142 000	1 020	1 625	2 110	2 506	2 836	3 115
142 001 - 144 000	1 033	1 645	2 136	2 537	2 871	3 154
144 001 - 146 000	1 046	1 666	2 162	2 568	2 905	3 192
146 001 - 148 000	1 059	1 686	2 188	2 598	2 940	3 230
148 001 - 150 000	1 072	1 706	2 214	2 629	2 975	3 268
150 001 +	1 072	1 706	2 214	2 629	2 975	3 268
plus % of excess	0.71%	1.14%	1.48%	1.75%	1.98%	2.18%

Newsome and Gilbert
Form LF 1179 (7/90)

Ontario Court
(Provincial Division)

Ontario

Application
Page 1 of 2

Form 4

Court file no.
D1234

at _47 Sheppard Avenue East_

North York, Ontario M2N 5X6

address

Applicant(s) *If more than one applicant, give name and address for each*

Full name ANN ROBINS	Full name
Address for service *(street & number, municipality, postal code)* 22 VANITY LANE NORTH YORK, ONTARIO	Address for service *(street & number, municipality, postal code)*
Lawyer *(name, address and phone number)*	

Respondent(s) *If more than one respondent, give name and address for each*

Full name JACK ROBINS	Full name
Address for service *(street & number, municipality, postal code)* 55 SCOUNDREL CRESCENT NORTH YORK, ONTARIO	Address for service *(street & number, municipality, postal code)*

1. I ask for an order for the following

1a ☒ support for	Birthdate	1b ☒ custody of		1c	visiting rights to the following child(ren):

1a ☒ support for
1a-i ☐ me ►
1a-ii ☒ the following person(s):

1b ☒ custody of
1b-i ☒ the children listed in 1a
1b-ii ☐ the following child(ren):

1c visiting rights to the following child(ren):

Full name(s)	Birthdate(s)	Full name(s)	Birthdate(s)	Full name(s)	Birthdate(s)
MARY ROBINS	JULY 10, 1979				
MARK ROBINS	APRIL 8, 1982				

1d ☐ other - see next page, paragraph 5

2. I ask for an order for court costs including costs paid on my behalf by third parties, to whom I assign such costs collected.

3. There has never been any other court action for divorce, annulment, alimony, maintenance, support, custody, access, division of property, possession of the matrimonial home or contents, a restraining order or other matrimonial matters between the respondent and myself, or between the respondent and any person for whose benefit a claim is made in this Application, except: *(Give date, name of court, court file no., nature of case. If no other proceedings, state "None").*

NONE

4. The respondent has entered into the following written or oral agreement or understanding in respect of the claims made in the application: *(Give details. If no agreement or understanding, state "None").*

NONE

SAMPLE #8 — Continued

Newsome and Gilbert
Form LF 1179-2 (7/90)

Application
Page 2 of 2

Form 4 | Court file no.

5. I also ask for an order for the following: *(Specify)*

      NOT APPLICABLE

6. The grounds for this application are as follows: *(Give details of grounds. Attach an additional page if necessary, and date and sign it.)*

1. The Respondent and I were married on February 15, 1978.
   There are two children of the marriage namely Mary Robins born July 10, 1979, and Mark Robins born April 8, 1982.

2. Until January 10, 19 , the respondent lived with the children and myself in a three bedroom apartment located at 22 Vanity Lane in North York. On that day the respondent informed me that he wanted to be on his own for a while and he moved out of the matrimonial home. He has not returned since that time and is living with a friend at 55 Scoundrel Crescent, in North York.

3. Since the respondent and I separated, I have had physical custody of the children and have taken care of all their needs. The respondent has visited the children once or twice but has not shown particular interest in them. Under the circumstances, I believe that I should have legal custody of the children.

4. I have asked the respondent on several occasions for money to support the children but he has failed to provide me with any funds. The respondent has a good job at Acme Ironworks and is fully capable of providing child support.

5. The details of my financial circumstances are set out in my Financial Statement.

JUNE , 199-
_____
Date

Ann Robins
_____
Signature

ANN ROBINS

Where the applicant claims financial support or claims custody of a child, this form must be accompanied by a financial statement in Form 5.

SAMPLE #9
FINANCIAL STATEMENT
ONTARIO COURT (PROVINCIAL DIVISION)

Ontario Court
(Provincial Division)

at _____ 47 Sheppard Avenue East

_____ North York, Ontario
address

Financial Statement
Page 1 of 4

Form 5 | Court file no. D1234

I, _____ ANN ROBINS _____, of _____ 22 Vanity Lane, Apt. #609, North York, Ont. M1P 3W5
name / *(address for service - street & number, municipality, postal code)*

solemnly declare that details of my financial situation are accurately set out below, to the best of my knowledge and belief.

N.B.: REFER TO CONVERSION TABLE AND CONVERT EITHER TO ALL WEEKLY OR TO ALL MONTHLY FIGURES.

PART 1: INCOME

SOURCE OF INCOME	WEEK	MONTH	
Pay, wages, salary (before deductions)	$	$1316.00	1
Public assistance	$	$	2
Unemployment insurance Worker's compensation	$	$	3
Pensions	$	$	4
Rent, board received	$	$	5
Baby bonus (Family assistance)	$	$ 66.00	6
Support payments	$	$	7
Other (income from business, interest tips. etc.; attach financial statements)	$	$	8
Total income from all sources	$	$ 1382.00	9

PART 1(a): INCOME DEDUCTIONS

TYPE OF DEDUCTIONS	WEEK	MONTH	
Income tax	$	$ 87.00	10
Union dues	$	$	11
Unemployment insurance	$	$ 31.00	12
O.H.I.P., Blue Cross, etc.	$	$	13
Pension plans	$	$ 12.00	14
Canada Pension	$	$	15
Credit union loan	$	$	16
Savings plans	$	$	17
Other	$	$	18
Total deductions	$	$ 130.00	19

Subtract line 19 from line 9 = Take home pay = 1252 / per week or month 20

PART 2: EXPENSES - COLUMN A

		WEEK	MONTH	
FOOD	Groceries and household supplies	$ 320.00	$ 320.00	21
	Meals outside home	$	$ 20.00	22
	Clothing	$	$ 30.00	23
	Laundry and dry cleaning	$	$ 10.00	24
HOUSING	Rent or mortgage	$	$ 460.00	25
	Taxes	$	$	26
	Home insurance	$	$	27
	Fuel (heat)	$	$	28
	Water	$	$	29
	Hydro	$	$ 30.00	30
	Phone	$	$ 18.00	31
	Cable T.V.	$	$ 12.00	32
	Repairs and maintenance	$	$	33
	Other	$	$	34
HEALTH & MEDICAL	Insurance, O.H.I.P.	$	$	35
	Drugs	$	$ 15.00	36
	Dental care	$	$ 30.00	37
	Payment on debts	$	$ 85.00	38
	Total column A	$	$ 1030.00	39

Add line 39 and line 58 = Total expenses = $ 1476.00

PART 2: EXPENSES - COLUMN B

		WEEK	MONTH	
TRANSPORTATION	Public transit, taxis, etc.	$	$	40
	Vehicle operation, gas and oil	$	$	41
	Insurance and licence	$	$	42
	Maintenance	$	$	43
	Life insurance	$	$	44
EDUCATION	School fees, books, etc.	$	$	45
	Music lessons, hockey, etc.	$	$	46
RECREATION	Newspapers, publications stationary	$	$ 10.00	47
	Entertainment, recreation	$	$ 25.00	48
	Alcohol, tobacco	$	$	49
	Vacation	$	$	50
PERSONAL	Hairdresser, barber	$	$ 20.00	51
	Toilet articles (hairspray, soap, etc.)	$	$ 15.00	52
	Babysitting, day care	$	$ 300.00	53
	Children's allowances, gifts	$	$ 20.00	54
	Support payments	$	$	55
	Savings for the future (excluding payroll deductions)	$	$	56
	Miscellaneous	$	$ 20.00	57
	Total column B	$	$ 446.00	58

per week or month 60

101

SAMPLE #9 — Continued

PART 3: ASSETS

TYPE		DETAILS — IF SPACE NOT SUFFICIENT, USE SEPARATE SHEET	VALUE OR AMOUNT	
		STATE NATURE AND ADDRESSES OF PROPERTY AND OWNERSHIP		
REAL ESTATE	1	NIL	.	60
	2		.	61
	3		.	62
		STATE YEAR AND MAKE		
CARS, BOATS, VEHICLES	1	NIL	.	63
	2		.	64
	3		.	65
		STATE WHERE LOCATED		
HOUSEHOLD GOODS AND FURNITURE	1	22 VANITY LANE, APT. #609	4,000·00	66
	2		.	67
	3		.	68
		DESCRIPTION		
TOOLS, SPORTS HOBBY, EQUIPMENT	1	NIL	.	69
	2		.	70
	3		.	71
		STATE TYPE - ISSUER - DUE DATE - NUMBER OF SHARES		
BONDS - SHARES - TERM DEPOSITS - INVESTMENT CERTIFICATES	1	CANADA SAVINGS BONDS	800.00	72
	2		.	73
	3		.	74
		STATE NAME AND LOCATION ACCOUNT NUMBER		
BANK ACCOUNTS	1	TORONTO DOMINION BANK #2204	600.00	75
	2	22 MELON COURT	.	76
	3		.	77
		STATE TYPE AND ISSUER ACCOUNT NUMBER		
SAVINGS PLANS R.R.S.P. PENSION PLANS	1	NIL	.	78
	2		.	79
	3		.	80
		TYPE - BENEFICIARY - FACE AMOUNT	CASH SURRENDER VALUE ▼	
LIFE INSURANCE	1	NIL	.	81
	2		.	82
	3		.	83
		STATE NATURE AND LOCATION OF BUSINESS		
INTEREST IN BUSINESS Attach separate financial statements for each business	1	NIL	.	84
	2		.	85
	3		.	86
		STATE NAMES OF DEBTORS		
MONEY OWED TO YOU	1	NIL	.	87
	2		.	88
	3		.	89
		GIVE DESCRIPTION AND LOCATION		
OTHER ASSETS	1	JEWELLERY 22 VANITY LANE, APT. #609	2,000,00	90
	2		.	91
	3		.	92
		TOTAL ESTIMATED VALUE $	7,400 00	93

SAMPLE #9 — Continued

Form 5 | Court file no.
D1234

PART 4: DEBTS

IF SPACE NOT SUFFICIENT, USE SEPARATE SHEET

TYPE OF DEBT	CREDITOR	SECURITY	FULL AMOUNT NOW OWING	MONTHLY PAYMENTS	
BANK OR TRUST COMPANY LOANS			.	.	94
			.	.	95
			.	.	96
FINANCE COMPANY LOANS			.	.	97
			.	.	98
			.	.	99
CREDIT CARD LOANS	VISA		1 200 00	85 00	100
			.	.	101
			.	.	102
OTHER DEBTS			.	.	103
			.	.	104
			.	.	105
			.	.	106
			.	.	107
			.	.	108
TOTALS			1 200.00	85.00	109

PART 5: OTHER INFORMATION

1. The expenses shown in Part 2 of this form are for:

   ☐ me

   ☐ the following child(ren): *(Give name(s) and date(s) of birth)*
   MARY ROBINS BORN JULY 10, 1979; MARK ROBINS BORN APRIL 8, 1982
   ☐ the following other person(s): *(Give name(s) and relationship(s))*

2. My employer's name and address is:
   Toronto Dominion Bank
   25 Melon Court
   North York, Ontario

3. Attached to this form is a copy of my income tax return filed with the Department of National Revenue for the last taxation year, together with all material filed with it and a copy of any notice of assessment or reassessment that I have received from the department for that year. *(If no returns filed, state: "None filed")*.

4. I also attach a statement showing future material changes that may affect my income, expense, assets or debts. *(Strike out if not applicable)*

Sworn before me at the ___City___ of ___North York___

in the ___Municipality___ of ___Metropolitan Toronto___

this _10_ day of ___June___ ,19 ____ *JM Commissioner*
                           A Commissioner, etc.

Ann Robins
Signature
(This form is to be signed before a lawyer, justice of the peace, notary public or commissioner for taking affidavits.)

SAMPLE #9 — Continued

CONVERSION CHART — Monthly, Weekly

Page 4 of 4

M	W	M	W	M	W	M	W	M	W	M	W	M	W
		$ 600	$ 138.55	$1200	$ 277.15	$1800	$ 415.70	$2400	$ 554.25	$3000	$ 692.85	$3600	$ 831.40
		605	139.70	1205	278.30	1805	416.85	2405	555.40	3005	694.00	3605	832.55
$ 10	$ 2.30	610	140.85	1210	279.45	1810	418.00	2410	556.55	3010	695.15	3610	833.70
15	3.45	615	142.00	1215	280.60	1815	419.15	2415	557.75	3015	696.30	3615	834.85
20	4.60	620	143.15	1220	281.75	1820	420.30	2420	558.90	3020	697.45	3620	836.05
25	5.80	625	144.30	1225	282.90	1825	421.45	2425	560.05	3025	698.60	3625	837.20
30	6.95	630	145.45	1230	284.05	1830	422.60	2430	561.20	3030	699.75	3630	838.35
35	8.10	635	146.65	1235	285.20	1835	423.75	2435	562.35	3035	700.90	3635	839.50
40	9.25	640	147.80	1240	286.35	1840	424.90	2440	563.50	3040	702.05	3640	840.65
45	10.40	645	148.95	1245	287.50	1845	426.10	2445	564.65	3045	703.20	3645	841.80
50	11.55	650	150.10	1250	288.65	1850	427.25	2450	565.80	3050	704.35	3650	842.95
55	12.70	655	151.25	1255	289.80	1855	428.40	2455	566.95	3055	705.50	3655	844.10
60	13.85	660	152.40	1260	290.95	1860	429.55	2460	568.10	3060	706.65	3660	845.25
65	15.00	665	153.55	1265	292.10	1865	430.70	2465	569.30	3065	707.80	3665	846.40
70	16.15	670	154.70	1270	293.30	1870	431.85	2470	570.45	3070	708.95	3670	847.55
75	17.30	675	155.85	1275	294.45	1875	433.00	2475	571.60	3075	710.15	3675	848.70
80	18.50	680	157.05	1280	295.60	1880	434.15	2480	572.75	3080	711.30	3680	849.85
85	19.65	685	158.20	1285	296.75	1885	435.30	2485	573.90	3085	712.45	3685	851.05
90	20.80	690	159.35	1290	297.90	1890	436.45	2490	575.05	3090	713.60	3690	852.20
95	21.95	695	160.50	1295	299.05	1895	437.60	2495	576.20	3095	714.75	3695	853.35
100	23.10	700	161.65	1300	300.25	1900	438.75	2500	577.35	3100	715.90	3700	854.50
105	24.25	705	162.80	1305	301.40	1905	439.90	2505	578.50	3105	717.10	3705	855.65
110	25.40	710	163.95	1310	302.55	1910	441.10	2510	579.65	3110	718.25	3710	856.80
115	26.55	715	165.10	1315	303.70	1915	442.25	2515	580.80	3115	719.40	3715	857.95
120	27.70	720	166.25	1320	304.85	1920	443.40	2520	581.95	3120	720.55	3720	859.15
125	28.85	725	167.40	1325	306.00	1925	444.55	2525	583.15	3125	721.70	3725	860.30
130	30.00	730	168.55	1330	307.15	1930	445.70	2530	584.30	3130	722.85	3730	861.45
135	31.20	735	169.70	1335	308.30	1935	446.85	2535	585.45	3135	724.00	3735	862.60
140	32.35	740	170.85	1340	309.45	1940	448.00	2540	586.60	3140	725.15	3740	863.75
145	33.50	745	172.05	1345	310.60	1945	449.15	2545	587.75	3145	726.30	3745	864.90
150	34.65	750	173.20	1350	311.75	1950	450.30	2550	588.90	3150	727.45	3750	866.05
155	35.80	755	174.35	1355	312.95	1955	451.45	2555	590.05	3155	728.60	3755	867.20
160	36.95	760	175.50	1360	314.10	1960	452.60	2560	591.20	3160	729.75	3760	868.35
165	38.10	765	176.65	1365	315.30	1965	453.75	2565	592.35	3165	730.90	3765	869.50
170	39.25	770	177.80	1370	316.45	1970	454.90	2570	593.50	3170	732.10	3770	870.65
175	40.40	775	178.95	1375	317.60	1975	456.10	2575	594.65	3175	733.25	3775	871.80
180	41.60	780	180.15	1380	318.75	1980	457.25	2580	595.80	3180	734.40	3780	873.00
185	42.75	785	181.30	1385	319.90	1985	458.40	2585	596.65	3185	735.55	3785	874.15
190	43.90	790	182.45	1390	321.05	1990	459.55	2590	598.15	3190	736.70	3790	875.30
195	45.05	795	183.60	1395	322.20	1995	460.70	2595	599.30	3195	737.85	3795	875.45
200	46.20	800	184.75	1400	323.35	2000	461.85	2600	600.45	3200	739.05	3800	876.60
205	47.35	805	185.90	1405	324.50	2005	463.00	2605	601.60	3205	740.20	3805	877.75
210	48.50	810	187.05	1410	325.65	2010	464.20	2610	602.75	3210	741.35	3810	878.90
215	49.65	815	188.20	1415	326.80	2015	465.35	2615	603.90	3215	742.50	3815	881.05
220	50.80	820	189.40	1420	327.95	2020	466.50	2620	605.10	3220	743.65	3820	882.20
225	51.95	825	190.55	1425	329.10	2025	467.65	2625	606.25	3225	744.80	3825	883.35
230	53.10	830	191.70	1430	330.25	2030	468.80	2630	607.40	3230	745.95	3830	884.50
235	54.30	835	192.85	1435	331.40	2035	470.00	2635	608.55	3235	747.10	3835	885.65
240	55.45	840	194.00	1440	332.55	2040	471.15	2640	609.70	3240	748.25	3840	886.80
245	56.60	845	195.15	1445	333.70	2045	472.30	2645	610.85	3245	749.40	3845	887.95
250	57.75	850	196.30	1450	334.85	2050	473.45	2650	612.00	3250	750.55	3850	889.15
255	58.90	855	197.45	1455	336.00	2055	474.60	2655	613.15	3255	751.70	3855	890.30
260	60.05	860	198.60	1460	337.15	2060	475.75	2660	614.30	3260	752.85	3860	891.45
265	61.20	865	199.75	1465	338.30	2065	476.90	2665	615.45	3265	754.05	3865	892.60
270	62.35	870	200.90	1470	339.45	2070	478.05	2670	616.60	3270	755.20	3870	893.75
275	63.50	875	202.05	1475	340.65	2075	479.20	2675	617.75	3275	756.35	3875	894.90
280	64.65	880	203.25	1480	341.80	2080	480.35	2680	618.90	3280	757.50	3880	896.10
285	65.80	885	204.40	1485	342.95	2085	481.50	2685	620.10	3285	758.65	3885	897.25
290	67.00	890	205.55	1490	344.10	2090	482.65	2690	621.25	3290	759.80	3890	898.40
295	68.15	895	206.70	1495	345.25	2095	483.80	2695	622.40	3295	760.95	3895	899.55
300	69.30	900	207.85	1500	346.40	2100	484.95	2700	623.55	3300	762.10	3900	900.60
305	70.45	905	209.00	1505	347.55	2105	486.15	2705	624.70	3305	763.25	3905	901.75
310	71.60	910	210.15	1510	348.75	2110	487.30	2710	625.85	3310	764.40	3910	902.90
315	72.75	915	211.30	1515	349.90	2115	488.45	2715	627.00	3315	765.55	3915	904.15
320	73.90	920	212.45	1520	351.05	2120	489.60	2720	628.15	3320	766.70	3920	905.30
325	75.05	925	213.60	1525	352.20	2125	490.75	2725	629.30	3325	767.85	3925	906.45
330	76.20	930	214.75	1530	353.35	2130	491.90	2730	630.45	3330	769.05	3930	907.60
335	77.35	935	215.90	1535	354.50	2135	493.10	2735	631.32	3335	770.20	3935	908.75
340	78.50	940	217.05	1540	355.65	2140	494.25	2740	632.80	3340	771.35	3940	909.90
345	79.65	945	218.25	1545	356.80	2145	495.40	2745	633.95	3345	772.50	3945	911.10
350	80.80	950	219.40	1550	357.95	2150	496.55	2750	635.10	3350	773.65	3950	912.25
355	81.95	955	220.55	1555	359.10	2155	497.70	2755	636.25	3355	774.80	3955	913.40
360	83.15	960	221.70	1560	360.25	2160	498.85	2760	637.40	3360	775.95	3960	914.55
365	84.30	965	222.85	1565	361.40	2165	500.00	2765	638.55	3365	777.15	3965	915.70
370	85.45	970	224.00	1570	362.60	2170	501.15	2770	639.70	3370	778.30	3970	916.85
375	86.60	975	225.15	1575	363.75	2175	502.30	2775	640.85	3375	779.45	3975	918.00
380	87.75	980	226.30	1580	364.90	2180	503.45	2780	642.05	3380	780.60	3980	919.15
385	88.90	985	227.45	1585	366.05	2185	504.60	2785	643.20	3385	781.75	3985	920.30
390	90.05	990	228.65	1590	367.20	2190	505.75	2790	644.35	3390	782.90	3990	921.45
395	91.20	995	229.80	1595	368.35	2195	506.90	2795	645.50	3395	784.05	3995	922.60
400	92.40	1000	230.95	1600	369.50	2200	508.10	2800	646.65	3400	785.20	4000	923.75
405	93.55	1005	232.10	1605	370.65	2205	509.25	2805	647.80	3405	786.35		
410	94.70	1010	233.25	1610	371.80	2210	510.40	2810	648.95	3410	787.50		
415	95.85	1015	234.40	1615	372.95	2215	511.55	2815	650.10	3415	788.65		
420	97.00	1020	235.55	1620	374.15	2220	512.65	2820	651.25	3420	789.80		
425	98.15	1025	236.70	1625	375.30	2225	513.80	2825	652.40	3425	790.95		
430	99.30	1030	237.85	1630	376.45	2230	514.95	2830	653.55	3430	792.15		
435	100.45	1035	239.05	1635	377.60	2235	516.15	2835	654.70	3435	793.30		
440	101.60	1040	240.20	1640	378.75	2240	517.30	2840	655.85	3440	794.45		
445	102.75	1045	241.35	1645	379.90	2245	518.45	2845	657.05	3445	795.60		
450	103.90	1050	242.50	1650	381.05	2250	519.60	2850	658.20	3450	796.75		
455	105.05	1055	243.65	1655	382.20	2255	520.75	2855	659.35	3455	797.90		
460	106.20	1060	244.80	1660	383.35	2260	521.90	2860	660.50	3460	799.05		
465	107.40	1065	245.95	1665	384.50	2265	523.10	2865	661.65	3465	800.20		
470	108.55	1070	247.10	1670	385.65	2270	524.25	2870	662.80	3470	801.35		
475	109.70	1075	248.25	1675	386.80	2275	525.40	2875	663.95	3475	802.50		
480	110.85	1080	249.40	1680	388.00	2280	526.55	2880	665.10	3480	803.65		
485	112.00	1085	250.55	1685	389.15	2285	527.70	2885	666.25	3485	804.80		
490	113.15	1090	251.70	1690	390.30	2290	528.85	2890	667.45	3490	805.95		
495	114.30	1095	252.85	1695	391.45	2295	530.00	2895	668.60	3495	807.15		
500	115.50	1100	254.05	1700	392.60	2300	531.15	2900	669.75	3500	808.30		
505	116.65	1105	255.20	1705	393.75	2305	532.30	2905	670.90	3505	809.45		
510	117.80	1110	256.35	1710	394.90	2310	533.50	2910	672.05	3510	810.60		
515	118.95	1115	257.50	1715	396.05	2315	534.65	2915	673.20	3515	811.75		
520	120.10	1120	258.65	1720	397.20	2320	535.80	2920	674.35	3520	812.90		
525	121.25	1125	259.80	1725	398.35	2325	536.95	2925	675.50	3525	814.10		
530	122.40	1130	260.95	1730	399.50	2330	538.10	2930	676.65	3530	815.25		
535	123.55	1135	262.10	1735	400.70	2335	539.25	2935	677.80	3535	816.40		
540	124.70	1140	263.30	1740	401.85	2340	540.40	2940	679.00	3540	817.55		
545	125.85	1145	264.45	1745	403.00	2345	541.55	2945	680.15	3545	818.70		
550	126.00	1150	265.60	1750	404.15	2350	542.70	2950	681.30	3550	819.85		
555	127.15	1155	266.75	1755	405.30	2355	543.85	2955	682.45	3555	821.05		
560	129.30	1160	267.90	1760	406.45	2360	545.05	2960	683.60	3560	822.20		
565	130.45	1165	269.05	1765	407.60	2365	546.20	2965	684.75	3565	823.35		
570	131.60	1170	270.20	1770	408.75	2370	547.35	2970	685.90	3570	824.50		
575	132.75	1175	271.35	1775	409.90	2375	548.50	2975	687.05	3575	825.65		
580	133.90	1180	272.50	1780	411.10	2380	549.65	2980	688.20	3580	826.80		
585	135.05	1185	273.65	1785	412.25	2385	550.80	2985	689.35	3585	827.95		
590	136.20	1190	274.80	1790	413.40	2390	551.95	2990	690.50	3590	829.10		
595	137.35	1195	275.95	1795	414.55	2395	553.10	2995	691.70	3595	830.25		

Page 4 of 4

SAMPLE #10
ORDER (SUPPORT AND CUSTODY)

Newsome and Gilbert
Form LF 1193 (7/90)

Ontario Court
(Provincial Division)

Order
Page 1 of 2

at 47 Sheppard Avenue East

Form 14 | Court file no.
D1234

North York, Ontario M2N 5X6

address

Judge

STERN

Date of order

Applicant(s) *if more than one applicant, give name and address for each.*

Full name	Full name
ANN ROBINS	
Address for service *(street & number, municipality, postal code)* 22 VANITY LANE	Address for service *(street & number, municipality, postal code)*
NORTH YORK, ONTARIO	
Lawyer *(name, address and phone number)*	

Respondent(s) *if more than one respondent, give name & address and lawyer details for each.*

Full name	Full name
JACK ROBINS	
Address for service *(street & number, municipality, postal code)* 55 SCOUNDREL CRESCENT	Address for service *(street & number, municipality, postal code)*
NORTH YORK, ONTARIO	
Lawyer *(name, address and phone number)*	Lawyer *(name, address and phone number)*

On *(motion or application)*   APPLICATION

of *(name)*   ANN ROBINS,

in the presence of *(parties and solicitors in court)*
ANN ROBINS, no one appearing for Jack Robins although he was
served with the Notice of Hearing and Application,

on reading the *(list documents filed on motion or application)*
Application and Financial Statement of Ann Robins,

and on receiving evidence and hearing submissions on behalf of *(name)*   ANN ROBINS

This court orders that:

1. Ann Robins shall have custody of Mary Robins, born July 10,
1979, and Mark Robins, born April 8, 1982.

2. Commencing on the first day of July 199- and on the first day
of the month thereafter, Jack Robins shall pay Ann Robins child
support for Mary Robins and Mark Robins, fixed in the sum of $200
per child per month.

3. Unless this order is withdrawn from the Office of the
Director, Family Support Plan, it shall be enforced by the
Director and the amounts owing under the Order shall be paid to
the Director who shall pay them to the person to whom they are
owed.

_____
Date of signature

_____
Signature of judge or clerk of the court.

105

A year after the order is made, you are laid off and cannot find other work. Your only source of income is $1 000 per month from unemployment insurance, which does not even cover your basic living expenses. Under these circumstances, you think you should be excused from making all or part of your support payments until your financial situation improves.

The law deals with this situation by allowing either party to a support order to apply to court to have the order varied. The court has broad power to vary the order, which includes the right to increase or reduce the monthly payments, to suspend payments, or to cancel any arrears.

The important point to remember about an application to vary is that the court will not conduct a rehearing of the original case. The applicant must show that there has been a material change in circumstances since the original order was made or that new evidence has become available that justifies the change requested.

Common situations that may justify a variation are substantial increase or decrease in the income of one of the spouses, remarriage by one of the spouses, illness of one of the spouses, or a substantial and unforeseeable increase in the expenses of one of the spouses.

Unless an applicant receives special permission from the court, an application to vary cannot be made until six months has passed from the date of the original order or a previous request for variation.

2. Can agreements for support be varied?

If you are receiving support payments under a written domestic contract, the right to vary the support provision should be spelled out in the contract. If the agreement does not include the right to seek a variation, you may be stuck with the terms of the original agreement, no matter how much your circumstances have changed. However, if the support provision results in circumstances that are unconscionable, the court may disregard the provision and fix support on the basis of the principles described above.

3. Can support payments be indexed for inflation?

The purchasing power of support payments is often seriously eroded by inflation. A monthly support payment that was adequate three or four years ago may no longer cover the monthly expenses of the dependant. In order to deal with this the dependent spouse may apply to court to have the support payments indexed for inflation in accordance with the monthly increase in the Consumer Price Index, published by Statistics Canada.

The court is obliged to increase the support payments to match the rate of inflation unless the spouse making the payments shows that his or her income has not increased by a similar amount.

f. THE FAMILY SUPPORT PLAN

1. The purpose of the Family Support Plan

Once you obtain a support order, your spouse is required to make payments as set out in the order. However, in the 1980s, government statistics showed that up to 75% of outstanding support orders were not paid in full. This was called "a national disgrace," and the government of Ontario created a new plan to deal with collection of orders for support. The Family Support Plan has offices at 55 Yonge Street in Toronto and has been in operation since 1992.

2. How does the Family Support Plan work?

Under the Family Support Plan, support payments are automatically deducted from the salary or other income of the person paying support. At the time that the support order is made, the Court also makes a "support deduction order," which directs the employer (or other income source) to deduct the support payments from the person named in the order and remit them to the Plan. If the person changes jobs, he or she must notify the Plan of the name and address of the new employer and a new support deduction notice will be issued. Employers or employees who fail to comply with the requirements of the Family Support Plan may receive fines of up to $10 000.

If the support payor is unemployed or self-employed, he or she must make support payments directly to the Family Support Plan, which will then forward the payment to the recipient. If a payment is not received on schedule, the Plan will assume it has not been made and will begin to take enforcement action.

3. What are the advantages of the Family Support Plan?

There are many advantages to collection of support orders through the Family Support Plan. As long as the payor has a regular source of income, support deductions will be automatic and recipients will get their support regularly. If the support payments are not received, the recipient has the benefit of legally trained people who specialize in support enforcement, without having to pay the cost of a lawyer. In addition, the Plan is fully computerized and has access to government data banks containing information about the payor's address and place of employment. This information is essential, as it is impossible to collect money from someone who cannot be found.

4. How are support orders enforced?

(a) Garnishment

If the payor is an employee receiving a regular salary, the Family Support Plan can collect arrears of support by garnishment of the payor's wages. The Plan completes a request for garnishment in the Provincial Court district where the payor resides or carries on business. The clerk of the court will then forward a notice of garnishment to the payor's employer, under which 50% of the payor's wages must be forwarded to the Plan and paid toward the arrears of support.

In addition to garnishment of wages, it is also possible to garnishee money owing to the payor from any other source. This includes bank accounts in the payor's name, rent or mortgage payments owed to the payor, and (if the payor is self-employed) accounts receivable from his or her business. A garnishment remains in effect for up to six years from the date the notice of garnishment is served.

(b) Registration against land

If the payor is the registered owner of land in Ontario, the support order may be registered against the title to that land. Upon registration, the obligation to pay support under the order becomes a charge on the property. If the payments are not made, the property may be sold, and the proceeds applied to payment of the arrears in the same manner as a sale under a mortgage.

(c) Writ of seizure and sale

A writ of seizure and sale is a document issued by the court in which the support order was obtained. It may be directed to the sheriff of any county or district in Ontario. The writ instructs the sheriff to seize goods or land belonging to the payor, and sell them to satisfy the outstanding arrears of support. A writ of seizure and sale is most effective when the payor is the registered owner of land in Ontario.

Once the writ is filed in the sheriff's office, it forms a lien on the payor's land and will usually prevent a sale or mortgage of that land from being completed until the debt is paid in full. If you have already registered your support order directly against the payor's land, a writ of seizure and sale is redundant. However, it is a good idea to file the writ because it applies to any land in the district owned by the payor, and the payor may own land that you are unaware of.

For property other than land, such as a car, boat, or business inventory, the sheriff must receive written instructions to seize the property and provide the exact location of the goods. You also have to pay a deposit to cover the costs of seizure and sale. Before instructing the sheriff to seize and sell, careful enquiries should be made to ensure that the property is really owned by the payor and that there are no outstanding liens against it. If you direct the sheriff to seize property in which an innocent person holds a valid interest, you could be held personally responsible for the loss.

(d) Default hearing

If all other means of enforcing your support order are ineffective, the director of the Family Support Plan may require the payor to appear in the provincial court to explain the default. The payor will have to file a financial statement and submit to an examination of assets and means. The court will presume that the payor has the ability to pay the arrears, unless he or she produces evidence that this is not the case. Unless satisfied that, for valid reasons, the payor is unable to pay the arrears, the court may imprison him or her for a period of up to 90 days.

g. PARENT SUPPORT

Until 1978, there was no legal requirement for an adult child to support his or her parents. Nevertheless, many children did so out of a sense of moral obligation and repayment for the years during which their parents supported them.

In 1978, the Family Law Reform Act made it a requirement that every child who is not a minor provide support for a parent who cared for or provided support for that child. The amount of support is determined by the need of the parent and the ability of the child to provide support. Not surprisingly, the number of court applications by parents for support from their children are very few when compared to applications for child support or spousal support. Although the law is on their side, it seems that most parents are not comfortable about demanding money from their children and are not willing to go to court to enforce their rights.

8
CUSTODY OF CHILDREN

No lawsuit results in more bitterness and misery than a dispute over custody of a child. When a separation occurs, the spouses often view their children as spoils of war, which they must recover to prove victory over their opponent. The victims of this attitude are, of course, the children, who usually retain affection for both parents and are constantly being pressured to favor one over the other.

To avoid a great deal of heartache, parents who are separating should do everything in their power to reach a friendly agreement concerning custody of and access to their child or children. If they put aside their personal differences and honestly consider what is best for the child, their decision will usually be as good or better than the one a judge will impose on them if they fail to agree.

If there must be a custody dispute, the parents should at least ensure that the fight takes place outside the presence of a child. Derogatory references to the other parent should be avoided at all costs, and the child should be encouraged to maintain a positive relationship with both parents.

a. THE RIGHT OF CUSTODY

Custody and access is covered by the Children's Law Reform Act, a provincial statute passed in 1982.

While both parents live together, they are equally entitled to custody and they share the rights and responsibilities associated with custody. When the parents separate and the child lives with one of them without objection by the other, the right of the other parent to custody is suspended until a court order or separation agreement provides otherwise. In other words, if you move out and leave your child with the other parent, you cannot change your mind later and take the child back unless you obtain a court order.

Similarly, if your spouse moves out with the child and you do not object, you will have to apply to court if you wish to recover custody at a later date.

Temporary arrangements about custody and access must be made if a claim for custody is contested, because it can often take a year or more to reach trial. If the spouses cannot reach a temporary agreement, either one may apply to court for an interim order of custody or access, which remains in effect until the main application is dealt with at trial.

An interim order usually maintains the existing situation and does not change the custodial parent before trial unless it is absolutely necessary. An interim order can be quite important, because when the case reaches trial, the court often looks at the state of affairs under the interim order. If those arrangements were satisfactory, the court will be inclined to accept them on a permanent basis.

Although most custody disputes are between the parents of the child, anyone may bring an application for custody. For example, if a child has lived with an aunt or grandparent for a period of years, that person might want to apply for custody. The court may grant custody to the non-parent, although it is extremely rare.

Provision is also made in the Divorce Act for a person other than a spouse to join in the petition for the purpose of claiming custody of or access to a child.

b. JURISDICTION OF THE COURTS

An application for custody or access may be brought in the Ontario Court (General Division) or the Ontario Court

(Provincial Division). The application must be heard in the region or district where the child ordinarily resides.

If the child does not habitually reside in Ontario, the courts of Ontario will not accept jurisdiction except in special circumstances.

c. THE BEST INTERESTS OF THE CHILD

When a dispute over custody of a child comes before the court, the decision must be based solely on the best interests of the child. While this is an easy principle to state, it is far more difficult to apply in practice, as each person applying for custody will claim that his or her proposal is best for the child.

In order to provide the judge with some direction, the Children's Law Reform Act contains the following list of factors to consider in determining the best interests of the child:

(a) the love, affection, and emotional ties between the child and,

    (i) each person entitled to or claiming custody of or access to the child,

    (ii) other members of the child's family who reside with the child, and

    (iii) persons involved in the care and upbringing of the child;

(b) the views and preferences of the child, where such views and preferences can reasonably be ascertained;

(c) the length of time the child has lived in a stable home environment;

(d) the ability and willingness of each person applying for custody of the child to provide the child with guidance and education, the necessaries of life, and any special needs of the child;

(e) any plans proposed for the care and upbringing of the child;

(f) the permanence and stability of the family unit with which it is proposed that the child will live; and

(g) the relationship by blood or through an adoption order be-
     tween the child and each person who is a party to the appli-
     cation.

The court is also instructed not to consider the past
conduct of a person applying for custody unless the conduct
affects that person's ability to act as a parent of the child.

d. ASSESSMENT

A dispute regarding custody of a child often involves complex emotional issues, and a judge may feel ill-equipped to
make the final decision. It is therefore common for the court
to appoint one or more child care professionals to assess and
report to the court on what is best for the child. The assessment is generally performed by, or under the supervision of,
a psychiatrist or psychologist, who meets with all the parties
and the child over a period of time, conducts various tests
and studies, and forms an opinion about who should have
custody of the child. The findings and opinion are submitted
to the court in a written report. Although the recommenda-
tions in the assessment report are not binding on the court,
they are likely to be followed unless the court is given a very
good reason to do otherwise.

If you are involved in a court-ordered assessment, you
should make every effort to co-operate with the assessors and
to demonstrate your reasons for seeking custody. You are
very much on trial during an assessment; the impression that
you make will be reflected in the recommendation made to
the court.

e. WHAT IS JOINT CUSTODY?

In recent years, many child care professionals have suggested
that even after parents separate they should continue to have
joint custody of their child. Although the child necessarily
lives with one parent, the other parent in a joint custody
arrangement has generous visiting rights and participates in
the important decisions affecting the child. The child feels

that both parents remain part of his or her life, even after the separation.

The main problem with joint custody is that it requires the parents to co-operate with each other on a day-to-day basis and to recognize that the other parent is a fit person to have shared custody. As a result, the courts are not likely to order joint custody unless it is agreed to by both parents, and unless the court is satisfied that they have the spirit of co-operation necessary for joint custody to work. Where the court is faced with a dispute over who should have custody, joint custody is usually not an appropriate solution.

f. THE RIGHT OF ACCESS

A parent who loses the right to custody almost always acquires a right of access. Access includes the right to visit with the child and the right to receive information concerning the health, education, and welfare of the child. A typical access schedule includes visits on Sundays or every other weekend, plus an extended visit during summer and Christmas holidays. In most cases, a court order or agreement simply states that the other parent shall have "reasonable access" and leaves it to the parties to work out the details.

However, if the parties cannot agree or will not co-operate in making access arrangements, either party may seek an order for specified access. This order states specific times during each week or month when visiting rights may be exercised. While specified access has the advantage of certainty, it is not as flexible as reasonable access, and for this reason it should be used only when necessary.

Under the Divorce Act, the court may also require the parent with custody of a child to notify the access parent at least 30 days before changing the child's place of residence, and provide details of the move.

Sometimes the parent with custody is afraid that the other parent will not look after the child properly during the visit, or will not take proper steps to ensure the child's safety. These fears are often more imaginary than real. But if there is clear evidence that the other parent has acted recklessly or irresponsibly toward the child in the past, then an order of supervised access may be appropriate. Under such an order, the access would take place only in the presence of a responsible adult in whom the parent with custody has confidence.

Another alternative available is the type of service provided by the Lakeshore Area Multi-Service Project (L.A.M.P.) located at 185 5th Street in Toronto. Under this program, parents can visit their children in a controlled setting under the supervision and guidance of a trained social worker.

It is not common for a parent to be denied access altogether. However, if there is evidence that the parent is likely to abuse the child or expose the child to an immoral or dangerous environment, the court may make an order terminating the parent's right of access. In the case of an older child, the court may also deny access if the child expresses an independent and consistent desire not to visit the parent.

g. CAN CUSTODY AND ACCESS ORDERS BE VARIED?

Orders for custody and access are never final; they can always be varied if the court decides that the variation is in the best interests of the child. The court can also overturn any provision for custody and access in a domestic contract if the welfare of the child so dictates.

Accordingly, either parent may apply to court for an order varying the present custody and access arrangements. The applicant must show that there has been a material change in circumstances since the agreement or order, making the previous terms of custody or access no longer appropriate. In the case of custody, the death or serious illness of the parent with custody is an example of a material change that would support an application to vary the custody order in favor of the other parent or some other appropriate person.

Under the Divorce Act, an application to vary may be brought in the Supreme Court of any province in Canada where one of the spouses ordinarily resides. If this is not the court that made the original order, a certified copy of the variation order must be sent to the original court.

h. ENFORCEMENT OF CUSTODY AND ACCESS ORDERS

It is up to the parent named in an order for custody and access to enforce it. However, if the child can be located, enforcement of these orders is not usually difficult. If the other parent refuses to honor the custody or access order, the court may direct the sheriff or any police officer to apprehend the child for the purpose of enforcing the order. A parent who disobeys a custody or access order can also be found in contempt of court and be subject to a fine or imprisonment.

Enforcement is much more difficult when the parent without legal custody disappears with the child (commonly known as child-napping). The parent entitled to custody cannot enforce the custody order because the child cannot be located. If the other parent is still in Canada, he or she can usually be traced through government data banks. Access to these information sources is available to any person upon application to the court.

If you suspect that your spouse or ex-spouse is planning to illegally remove your child from Ontario, you may apply to the court for an order transferring your spouse's property to a trustee to be held as security for the return of the child. The court can also order your spouse to post a bond for the return of the child and to deliver his or her passport to the court for safekeeping. Such an order will only be made if the court is convinced that the child is in real danger of being illegally removed.

9

LAWYERS, MEDIATION, AND THE COURTS

a. LAWYERS

1. How do I choose a lawyer?

There is no secret method for choosing a good lawyer. You can use the same methods you would use in choosing any professional — a doctor, accountant, auto mechanic, or plumber. Begin by asking your friends and relatives if they can recommend anyone or warn you away from anyone. But keep in mind that, although your brother's lawyer may be good at real estate, he or she may have no experience in family law matters. There are so many areas of law that most lawyers specialize to a certain degree.

If you cannot get a recommendation, the Law Society of Upper Canada operates a lawyer referral service, which is advertised in the Yellow Pages. The referral service will provide you with the name and telephone number of a lawyer who claims to be experienced in family law matters and who has agreed to provide a half-hour consultation for free.

Once you have located a lawyer, make an appointment by telephone for the initial consultation. During your meeting, be sure to ask the lawyer for an estimate of the total fee to complete the services you need. Also enquire if he or she has the time to work diligently on your problem and respond to any questions you may have along the way. There is nothing more frustrating than hiring a lawyer who does not seem to be doing anything about your case or who does not answer your telephone calls. If the lawyer will not give you a satisfactory answer on these matters, go elsewhere.

From the initial meeting, you will have to decide whether you feel satisfied with your choice of lawyer. If so, tell the lawyer you would like him or her to act for you. If you decide you want to look elsewhere, thank the lawyer for his or her time and say you are going to think further about your problem. Continue looking until you find a lawyer you are happy with.

2. Preparing for a meeting with your lawyer

Before you see your lawyer, prepare for your meeting in writing. Write out your name, address, age, place of birth, children's names, and the names of all the other people involved in your problem with as much information about them, their work, and their living situations as you can. Then write out a brief history of your problem, how it came about, what happened, and what you want done.

The lawyer will also want to know details about your financial circumstances and those of your spouse. Use the financial statement shown in Sample #9 (chapter 7) as a guide. If you prepare a financial summary in advance, you will save a lot of time in the meeting. You will also have a clear picture of the situation in your own mind.

It is a good idea to gain some general knowledge about this area of law before you see the lawyer. You will then be able to discuss your problem more intelligently and provide the lawyer with appropriate instructions. Reading through this book is one way to get the background information you need about family law.

You can also phone the excellent telephone service provided by the Law Society, known as Dial-A-Law (947-3333 in Metropolitan Toronto). The operator who takes your call will connect you to a tape-recorded summary of the law in the area of your choice. There are more than 100 taped summaries available, and there is no charge for the service.

Do not go to see your lawyer until you have an idea of what you want and who is involved and have all the necessary documents and information. You will only be told to go away and come back when you have it all together. Every minute spent with the lawyer costs you money. Don't waste the lawyer's time and then blame the lawyer because the bill is high.

3. How much will a lawyer cost?

A lawyer has nothing to sell but time. He or she has no other product. Accordingly, the fee will reflect the amount of time that your case consumes: this means every minute spent on it, whether on the telephone, in the office, or in court. Everything that you can do to save time and everything that you can do for yourself will keep your bill down.

You will find that lawyers charge from $60 to $300 per hour depending on their experience, skill, and reputation. When you hire a lawyer for an hour, you hire the person, the staff, and the office. But in an hour, a good lawyer can accomplish a great deal. It will not take many hours in most cases for a competent lawyer to complete the job for you. If you choose an inexperienced lawyer because his or her hourly rate is low, you may not save much money because that lawyer may take longer to complete the job. If you are not satisfied with the results and later seek an experienced and more expensive lawyer to rectify matters, it can end up costing much more than if you had chosen the experienced lawyer to begin with.

Many lawyers now employ paralegal assistants or law clerks who do routine legal work under the supervision of a lawyer, usually more efficiently and much less expensively. They have often taken various law courses and are familiar with the principles of law. Although they cannot practise law on their own, they can be of great assistance in minimizing the cost of legal services by working under the supervision of a lawyer. If your lawyer has a law clerk, feel free to consult the law clerk rather than the lawyer on simple matters. This way you can reduce the fee that the lawyer will charge you.

120

Most lawyers have a set fee for uncontested divorces, ranging from $400 to $850. A common fee is $600. You also have to pay court costs of about $325.

You should discuss the matter of fees and total cost with your lawyer at the outset. It may not be possible for your lawyer to give you an exact figure if there is a dispute involved — over children, property, or some other issue — because it is impossible to say how much time will be involved. Ask for a ballpark estimate based upon an hourly rate with an estimate of the number of hours.

Many lawyers are not prepared to wait to bill until the whole case is completed. Since a case can take a long time until it is completed, lawyers often send interim bills as the matter progresses. Feel free to discuss this with your lawyer before deciding to retain him or her.

Other lawyers ask for the fee in advance (usually called a retainer). It is usually not the full fee but a good portion of it. It is held in a special account, called the trust account, and used only for items such as court fees that must be paid on your behalf. The lawyer can use it only if he or she sends a bill to you setting out the details of the account. When you deliver the retainer, get a receipt.

Often the person seeking legal advice has no cash. Some lawyers will accept property as a retainer; others will work with little or no retainer. For example, where a wife is seeking help and there is a house in joint tenancy or a husband who is able to afford court costs if they are awarded, a lawyer may agree to act for her if she will turn over these proceeds at a later date. Talk to your lawyer about it and, if all else fails, consider legal aid.

Initially your lawyer should try to get your spouse to pay for the costs of the proceedings. These costs include a portion of your legal fees. However, to obtain costs, you have to adopt a reasonable approach about the conduct of the proceedings. In the courts that deal with family matters, there is provision made for each party to submit an offer of settlement to the other side. The judge will not see this at trial, but will look at it afterwards to decide who should pay the costs. If you have not made a reasonable offer of settlement, you probably will not get costs from your spouse even if you are successful. To make a settlement offer, you should be fully advised of your legal rights. Never try to make an offer without seeking the advice of a lawyer.

4. What if the bill is too high?

If a lawyer hands you a bill that you consider excessive or unfair, first discuss it with him or her to see if the amount can be justified. If you are unable to obtain any satisfaction in this manner, consider having your bill assessed. Assessment is a procedure for a client to have a lawyer's bill reviewed by an officer of the court who has the power to reduce the amount of the bill if it is found to be excessive.

In cases involving very large accounts, it is wise to retain a different lawyer to assist you. For small accounts, however, you can have the account assessed without a lawyer's help. If you live in Toronto, go to the Court office at 145 Queen Street West and ask for an order for assessment of costs. If you live outside Toronto, simply go to the nearest General Division Court office. Once the order to assess costs is obtained, the court office will give you an appointment with an officer of the court for assessment of the bill. After obtaining this appointment, mail or deliver a notice of appointment along with a copy of the bill being assessed to your lawyer.

On the appointed day, you should appear before the assessment officer and be prepared to explain in detail why you are dissatisfied with the account. The lawyer who sent the account will also appear to justify the account and to respond to your criticisms. The assessment officer will then decide on the appropriate amount you should pay. You are entitled to have your lawyer's account assessed even though you have already paid it, as long as you obtain your appointment within one month of the date of an itemized account.

Under special circumstances, such as fraud or gross excessiveness, you may have the account assessed even after the one-month deadline, as long as it is within 12 months of receipt. You should not attempt to do this without legal advice.

Be warned, as well, that your lawyer will not continue to represent you if you have the account assessed.

5. Other problems with lawyers

If a situation occurs with your lawyer that you consider improper or unfair, you can report the matter to the Law Society of Upper Canada, Osgoode Hall, Toronto, Ontario.

All complaints in writing to the Law Society are investigated. The Society may require the lawyer to forward to them for examination his or her file or at least the relevant portions of it. If there has been misconduct on the part of the lawyer, the Law Society will reprimand him or her. If the misconduct is more serious, the lawyer may be suspended or even disbarred.

6. Legal aid

Ontario has a legal aid plan that provides free legal services to those people who cannot afford a lawyer and who qualify under the plan. The lawyer's fees are paid directly by the legal aid plan to the lawyer.

If you need help, you must apply in person to your local legal aid office. You will be interviewed by an official about your financial situation as well as by a lawyer to determine the merits of your claim. If the officer decides that you are financially eligible and there appears to be merit in your case, you will receive a legal aid certificate. You may take this certificate within ten days to the lawyer of your choice, provided he or she will agree to act for you by accepting the legal aid certificate. If the lawyer agrees to act for you on this basis, he or she must submit all accounts to the legal aid plan.

The Legal Aid Act prevents a lawyer from charging any fee or disbursement to you directly.

Clients are frequently required to make some contribution directly to legal aid for their legal fees in situations where they have some income but not enough to pay the lawyer's full bill. If the client owns property, but has no money, legal aid will register a lien against the title to the property covering some or all of the estimated fees.

If you have retained a lawyer under the legal aid plan, you will be required to assign to legal aid any costs you are awarded if you are successful. If you recover money through a lawsuit funded by legal aid, reimbursement of the legal fees will be charged against the proceeds.

b. MEDIATION

1. What is mediation?

Mediation is a process of negotiation in which a trained person helps a separating or divorcing couple resolve their family disputes. The mediator meets with both spouses and sometimes with the children to try to work out an agreement that is most suitable for the particular situation. When the agreement is reached, it can be incorporated into a domestic contract or a court order.

Mediation is an alternative to settling family disputes in court. For some time now, experts have recognized that the courts are not the best place to deal with family problems, particularly where children are involved. This is because the courts operate on an adversarial system in which one party wins and the other party loses. In an effort to win the court contest, members of the same family become bitter antagonists, often with their children stuck somewhere in the middle. In contrast, mediation seeks a solution to the dispute in which there are no losers. Rather, the parties are encouraged to negotiate on a friendly basis and come up with an agreement that everyone can live with.

In addition to saving emotional cost, mediation can save you time and money. If the parties co-operate with the mediator, an agreement can be reached more quickly than it would take for the dispute to work its way through the courts. Moreover, the cost of the mediator is usually considerably lower than the cost of two lawyers and court disbursements.

Mediation is a rapidly growing field and is quickly becoming an important aspect of family law disputes. Although mediation services are now available in all areas of family law, they are most commonly used where custody, access, and support are in dispute. If one or both parties to the dispute receive legal aid, you may make use of the excellent mediation service provided by the Legal Aid Plan.

2. What if mediation doesn't work?

If you and your spouse cannot reach an agreement during the mediation process, one of you can always apply to court to have the matter decided. For this reason, it is important to decide at the outset if you want your mediation to be open or closed. Open mediation means that, if one of the spouses goes to court, the evidence of the mediator is admissible and either party has the right to cross-examine the mediator about statements made and matters discussed during the mediation. In closed mediation, no evidence of anything said or discovered in the course of the mediation can be used in court.

The advantage of closed mediation is that the parties can feel free to say or do whatever they want during the negotiation process, without fearing that it will be used against them later. On the other hand, open mediation narrows the issues before the court and allows the court to benefit from any progress made in the mediation.

3. Legal recognition of mediation

In recent years, mediation has received recognition by both the government and the courts. Under the Divorce Act, every lawyer who acts on behalf of a spouse in a divorce proceeding has a duty to discuss the possibility of mediation with his or her client and to advise the client of the mediation facilities available. Mediation services are available in Toronto through the Provincial Court at 311 Jarvis Street and through the Ontario Court (General Division) Family Courts (see section **c.1.c.**). There are also private mediators located in most of the urban centres in Ontario.

The spouses may also ask the court to appoint an agreed-upon person to mediate any issue raised in the court application. At the end of the mediation, the mediator appointed by the court must file a report with the court and give a copy to each of the parties. If open mediation was agreed to, a full report is required containing anything that the mediator considers relevant, including statements made by the parties and the mediator's recommendation about resolving the dispute. If the mediation was closed, the mediator files a limited report that either sets out the agreement reached by the parties only or states that the parties did not reach agreement.

4. How do I obtain mediation?

Besides the mediation facilities available through the government or the courts, there are a large number of private practitioners providing mediation services. These people are usually psychologists or social workers who offer a wide range of services, including marriage counselling, mediation, and separation therapy. If you cannot locate a mediation service, your lawyer, doctor, or the clerk of the local family court should be able to assist you.

The cost of mediation services varies greatly. Court and government-based services are usually free. Private practitioners can charge anywhere from $20 per hour to $200 per hour, with the average fee being about $85 per hour. Some mediators will charge less than their normal rate when clients cannot afford the regular fee. If one or both parties to the dispute receive legal aid, you may make use of the excellent mediation service provided by the Legal Aid Plan.

c. THE COURTS

1. What courts deal with family law?

There are a number of different courts in Ontario, with overlapping jurisdiction or authority. A brief summary of each court and its jurisdiction over family law matters is given below.

(a) The Ontario Court (Provincial Division)

This court gets its name from the fact that its judges are appointed by the province of Ontario rather than by the federal government as is the case with the other courts. The Ontario Court (Provincial Division) is commonly known as the family court. It has branches in most cities in Ontario, including four locations in Metropolitan Toronto. The family court has control over matters of custody, access, spousal support, and child support, as well as child welfare matters, adoptions, and prosecutions under the Young Offenders Act. However, it does not have jurisdiction over applications concerning family property or the matrimonial home, which must be dealt with in the Ontario Court (General Division).

If your application concerns a matter within the authority of the family court, your best bet is to file it there, especially if you are not planning to use a lawyer. The family courts are relatively quick and informal, and the court staff will usually provide you with the required forms and help you fill them out. Many of the family courts also have a lawyer, known as a duty counsel, who is available for consultation at no cost prior to your case being heard.

(b) The Ontario Court (General Division)

Every region or district in Ontario has a branch of the Ontario Court (General Division). This court has jurisdiction over applications concerning custody, access, support, division of property, and the matrimonial home. It also has exclusive jurisdiction over divorce proceedings and applications for support, custody, and access under a divorce proceeding.

127

If you are involved in Ontario Court (General Division) matters other than an uncontested divorce, you should have legal representation. The procedure in these courts is quite complicated, and the court staff will not provide you with forms or help you complete them. Trials are quite formal and the rules of evidence are strictly observed.

(c) The Ontario Court (General Division) Family Court

The Ontario Court (General Division) Family Court was created in the late 1970s as an experimental court in which all family matters could be dealt with at the same time instead of being handled by different courts. While it has the same jurisdiction in family matters as the Ontario Court (General Division), it has the informal atmosphere of the family court. It also places an emphasis on counselling, reconciliation, and mediation, and it employs a trained staff for this purpose. Branches of the Family Court are located in Hamilton, Barrie, Kingston, London, and Napanee.

2. How does a case get to trial?

(a) Originating and responding to documents

Regardless of which court you are using, the case is begun by a written claim or application. This document must be prepared by you or your lawyer on the form prescribed by the court. It is then issued by the court clerk or registrar, who signs it and affixes the court seal. This document is then hand-delivered to the other party who is given a fixed amount of time to serve and file a written response.

These written documents, sometimes called pleadings, are important because they set out the subject matter that will be dealt with at the trial. If you claim something at trial that was not raised in your pleadings, the judge may disallow it for that reason.

(b) Examination for discovery

After the pleadings have been exchanged, an examination for discovery sometimes takes place. In this procedure one or both parties are examined under oath, and their answers are recorded by a court reporter. The purpose of the examination is to find out what evidence the opposing party is relying on to prove the statements in the pleadings and to weaken that person's case through cross-examination.

For example, a typical pleading by the mother in a custody application might state: "The child's father is reckless and irresponsible and cannot be trusted to properly look after the child." During examination for discovery, the mother would be asked to provide evidence (through specific examples) of the father's reckless or irresponsible behavior. If she cannot provide examples or the examples are not relevant to the father's ability as a parent, her claim will be weakened.

Examinations for discovery are frequently used in the Ontario Court (General Division). They are available in the family court with a judge's permission, but are not very common.

(c) Motions

A motion is a request to the court to make a preliminary or procedural order of some kind before the trial. A motion may be brought at any time between the beginning of the action and the trial itself. In family law matters, the most common type of motion is for interim custody or interim support. But there can also be motions to amend (that is, alter) a pleading, to add another person to an application, to request assessment or mediation, to rule whether a question asked during a discovery is permissible, and numerous other matters.

Motions are often quite technical and are usually brought by lawyers at a considerable cost to their clients. If your lawyer is bringing or defending a motion on your behalf, make sure that it is really necessary and cannot be resolved by a compromise reached with the other party.

(d) Pre-trial

A pre-trial is an informal meeting between a judge and the lawyers representing the two parties. The judge reviews the case with the lawyers, seeks to narrow the issues in dispute, and usually recommends a proposal for settlement. This recommendation carries a lot of weight since the judge could impose it on the parties if he or she were trying the case.

The lawyers discuss the judge's recommendation with their clients, who are then faced with the choice of accepting the recommendation or going on to trial with a different judge.

Some judges allow the parties themselves to attend the pre-trial meeting with their lawyer. The meeting then takes the form of an impromptu mediation session, with the judge functioning as mediator. These meetings are often successful, and many disputes are resolved this way without the need for a trial.

(e) Trial

In contrast to a pre-trial, a trial is quite a formal affair. The purpose of a trial is to present the facts supporting your request. You do this through your sworn oral testimony and the submission of relevant documents.

Before giving evidence at trial, take some time to think about what you are going to say and how you will explain your side of the story to the judge. Remember the judge has not heard any part of the case and knows nothing about it, so you cannot assume he or she will understand your feelings. The judge must be told everything and made to understand.

The party bringing the application must call witnesses or personally take the witness stand and, once sworn to tell the truth, give evidence to the court. All evidence should be directed toward the judge and spoken in a clear voice so that everyone can hear. Don't speak too quickly, as the judge will want to make notes of what is said.

First, identify all the people involved. Be able to give the name, address, and date of birth of each of them. When discussing the children, dates of birth are necessary, and birth certificates are preferable. If a child is the child of your legal spouse or common-law spouse, say so. Don't expect it to be assumed.

Events are best described in chronological order. Try to be concise and detailed so that a complete picture comes out. Don't describe things in general terms; be specific whenever possible. For instance, saying that life with your spouse was unbearable will not help the judge understand your problem. Explain why it was unbearable by giving specific examples, such as: "He threw things at me at parties," followed by a list of the location and date of the incidents. Only that way will the court obtain a complete picture of the situation.

If there are any written documents, such as separation agreements, take the originals with you if possible. Prepare a list of your monthly expenses in writing, putting in totals and labels showing where the money comes from and where it goes. Make several copies of this list and take them to court with you so that it may be used as evidence in the trial, if necessary. The copies are for the defence, the plaintiff, the judge, and so on.

When you are on the stand, you should not refer to any written paper or other document without telling the court that you wish to do so. Only after you have permission should you use such aids.

Generally, you will not be allowed to say what someone else has told you (known as hearsay evidence). The reason for this is that you cannot give someone else's evidence; he or she must give it. The major exception to this rule involves anyone who is present in court. Since that person is able to deny any quote that is not accurate, you are allowed to repeat what he or she may have said to you. In matrimonial disputes this is often very important.

If you prepare well by going over the evidence before you go to court, you can relax in the witness box and give your evidence. Just say what happened and let the judge do the rest. Be sure to tell the truth; perjury is a very serious offence.

As each witness finishes giving evidence, the other party has an opportunity to cross-examine him or her on anything that has been said or on any other relevant matter that the witness knows about personally. While a witness is speaking, you should remain silent. If you have a question or challenge for that witness, make a note of it and pass it to your lawyer.

Once the party bringing the application has given evidence and called all the witnesses he or she intends to call, the other party is then entitled to give evidence and call his or her witnesses. Of course, as each witness finishes his or her evidence, the applicant or his or her lawyer is allowed to cross-examine and ask questions. After all the evidence has been heard, both sides are given an opportunity to tell the judge how they view the evidence and what they feel the judge's conclusion should be in the case.

After all the argument is in, the judge makes a decision. Occasionally, in more complicated cases, the judge adjourns the case after the argument and announces his or her decision at a later date. This is known as a reserved judgment.

(f) Appeals

In almost all cases, a judge's decision may be appealed, but there are strict time limits for bringing an appeal. If you wish to appeal any matter, contact a lawyer immediately. Appeals are complicated and difficult. They are also quite costly, so you should weigh the chances of success carefully before you proceed. Remember that the Court of Appeal will rarely interfere with the findings of fact made by the trial judge. As a general rule, a decision will not be reversed on appeal unless the trial judge made an error of law which results in a substantial miscarriage of justice to one of the parties.